THE CONDUCT OF AMERICAN FOREIGN RELATIONS

THE CONDUCT
OF AMERICAN
FOREIGN RELATIONS
The Other Side of Diplomacy

Thomas H. Etzold

New Viewpoints
A Division of Franklin Watts
New York | London | 1977

Library of Congress Cataloging in Publication
Data

Etzold, Thomas H
    The conduct of American foreign relations.

    Bibliography: p.
    Includes index.
    1. United States—Foreign relations—History.
2. United States—Foreign relations—1945-
3. United States—Diplomatic and consular service.
I. Title.
JX1407.E87   353.008′92   76-41285
ISBN 0-531-05390-3
ISBN 0-531-05597-3 pbk.

New Viewpoints
A Division of Franklin Watts
730 Fifth Avenue
New York, New York 10019

For Robert H. Ferrell,
who helped when I needed it

ACKNOWLEDGMENTS

Many institutions and people helped in the preparation of this manuscript. The Miami University (Ohio) Faculty Research Committee supported initial research into the conduct of American foreign relations. At the request of Professor Richard M. Jellison, Dean Clarence K. Williamson provided partial support for one visit to the State Department. Graduate assistants Nancy Armstrong and Steven Hurst labored in the library at Miami. Doris Baginski, reference librarian at the United States Naval War College, helped obtain source material. At Miami University, and especially at the Naval War College, Linda Gillespie, Agnes Gilman, Deanna May, Sara McKee, Ruth Saurette, and Louise Miller typed and retyped manuscript, and Mary Prasso smoothly supervised production of final copy.

A number of people in Washington assisted the work, though some of them I will not name, since this study may seem controversial to readers from the foreign affairs community. Milton Gustafson, chief of the diplomatic branch at the National Archives, assisted on this project as on so many others. So did his fine staff. William O. Hall, formerly director general of the Foreign Service, gave a long interview, as did one of his associates, Archer

Blood. Samuel Thompson of politico-military affairs, Norbert Krieg, William O. Franklin, Sven Groenings, Paul Kattenburg, John Bowles, Elwood Williams, Edward Rowell, William Trainor, Jr., Andrew Thoms, William Swing, the people of the Bureau of Public Affairs, and many others in the State Department and in the Central Intelligence Agency made visits instructive.

Teachers, colleagues, and friends aided with suggestions, readings, and criticism. Gaddis Smith years ago encouraged interest in the conduct of diplomacy. The members of the 1974–1975 faculty seminar at the Naval War College—David F. Trask, Richard Megargee, Craig Symonds, and Richard Harrison—read and discussed Chapter Three.

Jerry Holloway, a War College colleague and friend as well as a longtime Foreign Service officer, read the entire manuscript several times, always with suggestions for improvement. Barbara Nicholson, formerly of the Foreign Service Staff, read and criticized an early draft.

My wife, Suzanne Burdick Etzold, read many versions of the manuscript and discussed it and related problems in a most patient and helpful way.

Finally, Robert H. Ferrell, teacher, colleague, friend, patiently read and thoroughly criticized successive drafts of the manuscript. Without his efforts, the work would never have come to fruition.

T. H. E.

CONTENTS

THE CONDUCT
OF AMERICAN
FOREIGN RELATIONS

INTRODUCTION

The diplomacy that makes headlines in the world's newspapers—state visits, summits, conferences, famous names, and fast travel—comprises only one aspect of relations among nations. It is an important side of foreign relations, for from high-level meetings the high-level officials can issue statements and decisions that affect the destinies of many people. Justifiably, an air of excitement pervades the diplomacy of princes and presidents and helps to concentrate attention on the fascinations of state business at the grandest levels of pronouncement and policy.

But there is another side of diplomacy, less dramatic though no less important: the conduct of foreign relations. The business of states in the modern world possesses a complexity and breadth almost beyond description. Neither in times past nor in the present have governments been able simply to set out policy and then let relations take care of themselves. From the beginning of American experience the conduct of foreign relations has required the labor of many people, from the six-man department and the handful of representatives overseas in the time of the first secretary of state to the more than six thousand Washington-based employees of the State Department today and the additional thousands in nearly three hundred embassies and consulates around the world.

Whether with the few men of the original Department of State or the many of modern times, foreign relations take considerable organization. Neither the ideas to guide early foreign affairs nor a method of carrying them out came easily to rebellious colonials resolved on independence. In one of the great trials of the American Revolution the Continental Congress experimented, ceaselessly it sometimes seemed, to devise an organization adequate for foreign relations. Years passed before the elements of an organization appeared. Secretaries of state in the nineteenth century elaborated on the institutions of early constitutional days, and by the end of the century had done much to improve the department. By that time, however, Americans faced a new generation of problems, those associated with organizing the ever-growing diplomatic and consular services, in which tension had developed between the esprit of an informal elite and the demands for reform and reorganization that grew out of increases in the national business and in the size of the department and its staffs at home and abroad.

Personnel concerns of an enlarged organization predominated in the years after the turn of the century. Although Congress considered the requirements of organized foreign relations, the legislative landmarks proved insufficient—controversial guides through periods of expansion in the work of the department and in its bureaucracy. Desperation and hope increasingly drove people in Congress and the State Department to look for answers to the problems of work and organization with results that were equivocal.

Enlargement of the foreign affairs establishment concurrent with expansion of national interests and the nation's business during World War II brought near chaos to the organization. Not the least of the confusion was a romantic exaggeration of the historic influence of professional diplomats and secretaries of state. While members of the department had illusions about the past, their organization lost influence on policy and on foreign relations as new agencies carried on the work in war and afterward in peace, with the result that professionals of the Foreign Service and officials of the Department of State in Washington found themselves displaced in their own areas of competence and responsibility.

Only one important aspect of diplomacy has remained consistent through the difficult expansion of the organization in wartime and in postwar eras, namely, the life and work of a representative abroad. The challenges of life in a foreign country—and sometimes just the difficulties in getting there—call for people of unusual determination. And the traditional functions of diplomats as representatives and observers require that envoys be mature in judgment and demeanor, sensitive in intuition, and competent.

After two centuries the problem of organization in the Department of State and the Foreign Service, and consequently in American foreign affairs, remains unresolved. The great question is what to try now. The attentions of Congress, suggestions of secretaries of state, proposals of reformers, task forces, political scientists, have not as yet eradicated the difficulties. Perhaps there is no ready solution, or resolution, and certainly no one should expect that a great nation can discover a way to conduct foreign relations effortlessly and without fault. But it is not too much to hope for elimination of the weaknesses in American diplomacy in the late twentieth century. If the professionals can discover their purpose and strengths, and recognize their limits, the organizational problems will subside. When they do, the foreign relations of the United States will surely benefit.

CHAPTER ONE | Organizing for Foreign Relations: 1775–1924

The creation of machinery to conduct the foreign relations of the United States has proved to be one of the most time-consuming tasks in the history of American government, and it is not unfair to say that at the bicentennial the task is uncompleted, the mechanism not yet in order. The reasons why this should be so are not, however, difficult to comprehend. For one thing, the work of American diplomats abroad and of the officials of the Department of State in Washington is extraordinarily complex. No single department in the government has to deal with such a multiplicity of problems. For another, Americans from the outset have sought to design a mechanism of foreign affairs that would be responsive to the people, and this is no easy task. When American diplomats talk to their foreign opposites as if they represent the President, this is mere form, as they represent the American people. When they send home cables to the SecState (the secretary of state), that too is form. And yet the popular base of American foreign relations has tended to disappear from the minds of practitioners. To prevent such lapses, the mechanism continuously evolves.

Perhaps a third reason why the machinery of foreign relations proves difficult to arrange is that Americans live in a large country, a rich country, where their own interests easily can be occupied, and the temptation frequently has been to forget about foreign relations until something suddenly emerges, until a crisis is at hand—out of sight, out of mind. The machinery begins to move in inadequate ways, the people who are moving it become inefficient, and no one pays much attention until the fact of failure becomes overwhelmingly evident.

1| Revolution and Independence

At the outset of independence the task of organizing the new nation's apparatus of foreign relations was novel in the extreme, for want of almost any preliminary training or experience. The colonies of British North America had conducted no foreign relations in any official sense, even though trade, legal and illegal, had grown to international proportions. The increasing estrangement between mother country and colony after 1763 had sometimes caused relations with Great Britain to seem like foreign relations. That perspective was neither shared nor appreciated by the British. Late in Benjamin Franklin's service as a colonial agent in London the privy council chastised him for, among other things, behaving too much as though he represented a foreign state. One angry London critic described Franklin as having been so "possessed with the idea of a Great American Republic that he may easily slide into the language of a minister of a foreign independent state. . . . But Dr. Franklin, whatever he may teach the people at Boston, while he is here, at least, is a subject." [1]

Shortly after Lexington and Concord the Continental Congress nonetheless appointed a Secret Committee on Foreign Correspondence and charged it to communicate with persons abroad who might become friends of colonists in revolt. Franklin seemed a natural choice as chairman of such a committee, not just because of his long years in London (he had been there since 1757), but for his many attainments. Perhaps no other American could claim as wide a circle of acquaintance in Europe, and certainly no one else in the colonies could equal his international reputation as scientist, philosopher, essayist, wit, and raconteur.

The committee, however, proved an ineffective body. As a representative of the Continental Congress, it possessed an anomalous character. Because the Congress lacked sovereignty, committee members could at best conduct only informal diplomacy, although diplomacy, as a rule, is formal business indeed. The committee's circumstances produced still another difficulty. Between the outbreak of revolution and the appearance of the new government under the Constitution in 1789, Congress kept close watch over foreign relations, perhaps because it lacked power in domestic affairs. The Secret Committee on Foreign Correspondence labored under the flighty and sometimes meddling attentions of the legislators.

And as if the committee did not have sufficient problems, there was the very real danger that its duties might be duplicated by another committee. In 1776 the Continental Congress had 169 special and 14 standing committees, with no apparent end to proliferation in sight. Congress, in fact, appointed a special committee in December 1776 to devise a plan for obtaining foreign assistance and failed to include a single member of the secret Committee on Foreign Correspondence.

While organizing a mechanism at home it was necessary to send envoys abroad, and here Congress made a signal mistake at the outset; for important diplomatic missions it appointed not a single ambassador or minister, as was customary in the chancelleries of Europe, but commissions in which several representatives possessed equal rank. The reason was obvious enough; Congress felt that the representation of a republic abroad should reflect the interests of the republic at home, that is, should include envoys from at least the several sections—New England, the middle states, the South. But the resulting problems almost surpassed description; it was not long before quarrels among commissioners competed with the quarrels between the United States and Britain for congressional attention.

Such were the circumstances in which Franklin arrived in Paris in December 1776, for he had just accepted appointment as co-commissioner in the all-important mission to France in search of assistance vital to American hopes. He was joining Silas Deane, the first emissary to France, and Arthur Lee, who had preceded Franklin to Paris only a short time earlier. News of the American savant's appearance traveled before him and caused some stir because of his reputation. There also were, of course, the political implications of his arrival. The British ambassador, Lord Stormont, attempted to forestall his reception at court and threatened to return to England should the French government so much as permit the new envoy to enter Paris. The French minister's reply, penned two centuries ago, was delightfully subtle: Although His Majesty's minister, Charles Gravier Comte de Vergennes, had dispatched a courier to forbid Dr. Franklin to enter Paris, it was possible that the American would reach the city before the courier should find him; in that case the French government could hardly turn him away without presenting a scandalous scene to all France. For this would show that the French government was disrespectful of the laws of nations and of hospitality.

It was not long before the new American commissioner, so carefully received, found himself busy in the extreme. He was the object of adulation and enthusiasm, his face known to everyone by virtue of its appearance in portraits and on medallions. In his affected role as a poor Quaker and backwoods philosopher he engaged the hearts of the French and became such a celebrity that he could not venture into the street without spectators. Verily, as he wrote home with understandable satisfaction, Paris "idol-ized" him. The dour John Adams, at that time minister to The Hague, not particularly pleased with the deceptions practiced by the second richest man in America, remarked with some suspicion that the French people "seemed to think he was to restore the golden age." [2]

Franklin's reception was so enthusiastic that it aroused the jealousy of his co-commissioners, Deane and Lee. Overshadowed by their associate, they squabbled, and eventually Lee vilified

Deane so successfully that Congress would not pay his bills for expenses. The result was tragic for Deane. He lived out his last years in England, a deserter from the cause of independence. Though not everyone believed Lee's charge that Deane had profited from commissioning privateers and purchasing war supplies, his conduct in exile cost him his last friends. In 1784 he tried to see John Jay, who was passing through London on the way home from negotiating in Paris. Jay refused, writing that although he would have been willing to hear an explanation of Deane's conduct out of consideration for their earlier friendship, he had learned that Deane was on good terms with General Benedict Arnold. That was simply too offensive; Jay considered Deane polluted by such contact.

Franklin's appearance in Paris, then, led to a falling out among commissioners and the discrediting of Deane. During the Paris years Lee was less successful in undercutting Franklin, although he tried, for he had a strong desire to become sole minister to the French government. In letters to America he represented Franklin as senile, unable to carry on business, and in Paris abused him so intemperately that Franklin at last refused to answer letters or to speak to him. When Franklin could no longer tolerate the situation he wrote Congress asking whether it intended to keep three commissioners at Paris, who were, in fact, augmented by the unreceived minister to Tuscany, Ralph Izard, and about to be joined by an unreceived minister to Vienna. The expense of maintaining the several commissioners seemed to Franklin enormously great, and he doubted that the utility would equal the cost. He pointed to difficulties of finding men who could live in harmony with each other and their servants and wished that Congress would separate the commissioners. Whether because of such complaints, or because of fatigue with the constant unhappiness of the situation, Congress did simplify the Paris mission. With Deane recalled, it dismissed Lee, and Franklin became sole minister to France in 1778. The commission system, excepting for special tasks, had proven a clumsy mode for diplomatic representation.

As if American diplomatic representation did not have enough troubles in the early years, in the confusions of congressional committees and the commission system of representation abroad, there was another difficulty—the extraordinary reluctance with which men of republican principles and simple upbringing, such as John Adams, could make their way through the forest of tradition, of ceremony, and generally of formalism that graced and disgraced the courts of Europe in the late eighteenth century, the French court perhaps most of all. The brusque, undiplomatic Adams initially sought to ignore the civilities of Versailles when he arrived in 1780, counting his sheer lack of diplomatic experience as an advantage. His straightforwardness and especially his peremptory language so irritated the French foreign minister that the Count de Vergennes turned over Adams' correspondence to Franklin for transmission to Congress and refused to have anything more to do with him. Adams doughtily defended himself. Contrasting his tactics with those of "veterans in diplomatics," he described himself as similar to militia troops that "sometimes gain victories over regular troops even by departing from the rules . . . a man may give offense to a court to which he is sent and yet succeed." [3] Or so Adams thought, and in such manner he believed it appropriate to conduct himself.

Franklin, incidentally, had no trouble, and no qualms, about entering into the customs and perhaps even the debaucheries of the France of his time, and indeed it may have been knowledge of this behavior that made Adams so intractable as to become almost *persona non grata*. Adams had remarked that "No man will ever be pleasing at a court in general who is not depraved in his morals or warped from [his] country's interests." [4] The assertion bespoke more the perspective of an Adams than any principle of the diplomatic art, and Franklin dissented as heartily from it as could a man of seventy-three years. Franklin lived well, though probably not with extravagance, flattered the king and court, loved the customs, wine, and people. Not least, he loved the women of France. One of his notable female friends was the famous Madame Helvétius, and there were several others. He later would lament the inconclusive nature of his liaison with Madame Helvétius. Writing to her in the third person, he complained delicately: "As he has already given her many of his days, although he has so few of them left to give, it seems ungrateful in her that she has never given him a single one of her nights." [5]

A man of such grand and boundless spirit could not by personal qualities offset the weaknesses that afflicted the conduct of his country's foreign relations. Fortunately, neither Congress nor any of the "militia" representatives abroad were for long content with this state of affairs, and even before the alliance with France of 1778 the Secret Committee on Foreign Correspondence had given way to a successor.

The Committee for Foreign Affairs made its appearance in April 1777. In its very title it showed the difference that time had made in revolutionary circumstances. No longer a secret and perhaps illegal undertaking, foreign relations by 1777 had become legitimate and public business of the United States of America. And foreign relations were becoming a task not merely of a public nature but were being organized with care, for the committee's chairman was an official of prominence.

Although the new committee was more successful than the one it superseded, it proved not entirely successful, perhaps because of the personalities of its chairmen. The patriot Thomas Paine first served as secretary, but in the era of nation-building his temperament contributed less than it had in the era of agitation. Within two years he was forced to resign, technically for releasing secret information but actually as a result of his continual struggle against Congress for more authority for himself and the committee. Paine's pretension to being a foreign minister strained the patience of conservative members of Congress, to whom there was a difference between the post of foreign minister, which Paine craved, and that of secretary to the Committee for Foreign Affairs, which he possessed. Under Paine's successor, James Lovell, the committee system admittedly showed little sign of improvement. As Lovell said, "there is really no such thing as a Committee of foreign affairs existing, no Secretary or Clerk, further than I persevere to be one and the other." [6] He could not keep up with the correspondence—perhaps not entirely his fault in a day when everything had to be written and copied by hand, when the typewriter and carbon paper were far in the future.

Then at last Congress made another emendation in the arrangement of American foreign relations, a change that lasted until the organization of government under the Constitution. In 1781, when the Articles of Confederation went into effect, there appeared the Department of Foreign Affairs. Congress had ordered the Committee for Foreign Affairs to study the ways in which other governments conducted diplomatic matters. It was no surprise that the committee found the best models in the bureaucracies of the greatest powers of the day (who wants to emulate a minor power?). Although Americans did not copy the French system, which like the British featured a powerful minister with influence on policy, they attempted to approach such a system. In replacing the Committee for Foreign Affairs, Congress deliberated, delayed, and finally chose a middle course, less than thoroughgoing reform but more than a mere continuation of the unsatisfactory arrangement that was then in operation. To head the new Department of Foreign Affairs, Congress appointed a secretary who would be more than a clerk in charge of correspondence but less than a foreign minister in the European mode. Although he could attend Congress to listen and learn that body's sentiments and intentions he could not ask questions or explain his views. The secretary was to correspond with ministers abroad and receive correspondence or communications from representatives of foreign governments resident in the United States. He possessed no latitude in foreign affairs and suffered, as had his predecessors, from the congressional inclination to correspond directly with ministers and carry on foreign relations through committees unrelated to the new department and its secretary.

It is perhaps worth pointing out that the first secretary for foreign affairs, Robert R. Livingston, found the disadvantages of the position too frustrating to offset the honor and resigned the office in June 1783. Only by chance did Congress escape serious consequences from its subsequent delay in replacing him. The republic failed to find a successor to Livingston during the crucial year in which peace with Britain was negotiated. In some of the most important months of the struggle for independence the new nation had no individual to oversee foreign affairs. Even Livingston's assistant had resigned because Congress withheld authority and relied on committees and fortuitous international circumstances and the high abilities of the few good men working in Paris. Franklin's charm and easy relations with the French, Adams' tenacity, and Jay's acumen and legal talent for advocacy combined to seize the diplomatic advantage amid rivalries between the governments in Paris and London. Even so, all of the American talents and favorable circumstances might not have sufficed to provide so brilliantly successful a peace as the Treaty of Paris of 1783 had it not been for the brief tenure of Lord Shelburne in the British Foreign Ministry. His friendship for American aspirations helped the government of George III agree to the treaty and cost him his cabinet position, because of the reaction of colleagues to his apparent overgenerosity.

Shortly thereafter a new secretary for foreign affairs, Jay, took office and finally held control of the country's foreign relations until the Constitution went into effect in 1789. Jay actually remained as acting secretary of state under the new government until Thomas Jefferson could return from Paris, where he had been minister, to take the first cabinet office in 1790. The adroit New Yorker had cleverly set conditions before accepting appointment in 1784. Only if Congress would establish a permanent seat of government, only if he could appoint his own clerks, would he take the post. In office, he forced Congress to a careful definition of responsibilities of the secretary and held tight control over his department. Congress in 1785 agreed that all communications on foreign relations should pass through the secretary and permitted him to determine Adams' instructions as first American minister to England. In addition, Congress authorized Jay to meet with a special envoy from Spain to negotiate a commercial treaty. No other American influenced the future institutions of his country's foreign affairs as did Jay during the 1780s. His accomplishments in centralizing control, his success in making the secretary an advocate of policy, and eventually his arguments in *The Federalist* in favor of a strong central agency for foreign relations—all these actions profoundly affected the future. His ability and fidelity to the public trust removed the suspicions of partisanship that had impeded his predecessors, and his competence in office manifested the efficiency and stability so much sought as Americans outgrew the era of half measures and under the great document of 1787 entered an era of increasing confidence at home and abroad.

2| Nineteenth Century

No one could have foreseen the ways in which the Department of Foreign Affairs would be transformed, would change its duties and outlook and take on increasing importance, under the constitutional government inaugurated in 1789. Although the Constitution did not establish executive departments, it assumed their necessity, and Congress in mid-1789 considered what agencies the new executive would require to carry out responsibilities and exercise powers. After prolonged debate it created departments of foreign affairs, war, and treasury, with precedence to foreign affairs. In general, the new department and its secretaryship resembled the institution under the Articles of Confederation, but with the important difference that the secretary for the Department of Foreign Affairs was responsible to the President, not Congress, and could act without consent of the Senate, an important addition to the power of the President and to the independence of the secretary. But the original and attractive simplicity of the arrangement lasted barely six weeks, and Congress, in September 1789, changed the name to Department of State. Again feeling its way through the maze of problems and tasks that fell to a new government, Congress had discovered functions that did not fall into any of the three main departments. Rather than create a bureaucracy, it assigned the duties to the Department of Foreign Affairs and changed the department's name. The secretary of state became responsible for a surprising variety of tasks. He took possession of the Great Seal of the United States, issued patents, received for copyright all books, maps, charts, and musical compositions produced in the United States, preserved the correspondence of the President, published federal laws and treaties, corresponded for the President with the governors of the states, published census returns, received petitions for executive pardon, directed territorial affairs, and signed and recorded land patents. At times the secretary of state managed the mint, kept records on the impressment of seamen, controlled the immigration service, published annual reports and records of commercial relations, and issued letters of marque and reprisal. The secretary, of course, also advised the President on foreign policy and carried on the work of foreign relations. Gradually the diplomatic business of the Department of State increased, and most of the tasks extraneous to foreign relations were reassigned to other executive departments.

In setting out the organizational changes of the mechanism of foreign affairs it is important to show the individual contributions of some of the notable secretaries of the nineteenth century. John Quincy Adams became secretary in 1817, at a time when the strains of national growth were intensely affecting the department, and he contributed much to the department and to foreign relations. He was appointed to balance the administration geographically and politically, not primarily because of his personal merit. Undaunted, he bent his dedicated abilities and stamina to the task of his office. He improved almost every aspect of the department's work, not always with the support of Congress. In 1821 when Congress was interested in cutting costs, someone thought of reducing the appropriation for foreign affairs. Secretary Adams saved the day by explaining to an inquiring senator why the Department of State was spending twice as much money in 1820 as it had in 1800. He enumerated the increased demands on the department occasioned by the expansion of the Union and by the consequent increase in members of Congress with their inquiries and other needs, and demonstrated that the salaries of the department, from the secretary's to the lowest clerk's were all inadequate.

Adams' tenure was an important era in the department's development. Although no other American of his time could have boasted the length or variety of his diplomatic experience, he possessed few of the personal qualities commonly associated with the diplomatic art. He once wrote: "I am a man of reserved, cold, austere, and forbidding manners; my political adversaries say, a gloomy misanthropist, and my personal enemies, an unsocial savage. With a knowledge of the actual defect in my character I have not the pliability to reform it." [7] Yet Adams' accomplishments in 1817–1825 entitle him to stand among the most important secretaries of state. He deplored the lack of a filing system in the department and instituted a continuing record of incoming documents, together with a system of indexing and summarizing diplomatic and consular correspondence. By defining salaries and responsibilities of the department's clerks, assigning consular correspondence to one, passports and ciphers and other duties to another, he brought order to a department grown inefficient.

Some of the deficiencies Adams found in the department, and some of the improvements he made in consequence, excite amazement at the ability of his predecessors to carry on foreign relations at all. The library of the Department of State, by virtue of careless administration, many moves, fires, and the depredations of the British in 1814, had become useless. Even though the department had recently moved into new quarters, the library had not been put in order. Adams personally designated space for the library, ordered the shelves, and established a charge-out loan system so that volumes did not simply disappear and in addition provided basic references for the daily tasks of the department by acquiring copies of statutes of the various states and of laws enacted in legislative sessions.

It is interesting to note that in several areas of work now remote from the tasks of the Department of State, Adams also made lasting impressions. Under his direction the census of 1820, for which the State Department was responsible, became the most thorough and well-prepared yet undertaken. From 1817 to 1821 he worked on studies and recommendations on the standardization of weights and measures, and his report served for many years as the standard American reference.

Another notable organizer of American foreign relations followed closely on Adams. Louis McLane, Andrew Jackson's first secretary of state, made reforms in 1833 that had considerable influence on the structure of the department. His reorganization constituted the first thorough revamping of the department since 1789. He improved markedly on the good work of Adams, who had defined responsibilities of clerks so that there would always be someone to perform each duty in the department. McLane devised a system of seven bureaus: diplomatic; consular; home, archives, laws, and commissions; pardons; remissions, copyrights, and library; disbursing and superintending; translating and miscellaneous. He subdivided the diplomatic bureau into geographical sections, foreshadowing the present-day department organization. He set a no-nonsense tone in the department by announcing work hours of 10:00 A.M. to 3:00 P.M. each weekday, during which no clerk could be absent without excuse. Department papers were classified confidential. He enjoined the staff to dispose of all business on the same day it was put before them.

Adams and McLane were the major innovators during the nineteenth century, and for the most part other improvements and refinements in the diplomatic institutions of the United States came in small changes by discontented secretaries or an aroused Congress. The latter body in 1853 created the position of assistant secretary of state, an innovation long sought by secretaries, won at last by the three-time secretary of state, Daniel Webster. Three years later Congress established a new system of ranking and classifying clerks in the department, supplementing an act of the previous year that had defined the rank of the many diplomatic and consular posts, fixed salaries for grades of diplomatic and consular officers, and eliminated the questionable practice by which consuls received no salary and lived from commissions and fees received for performing their duties. For fifty years the acts of 1855 and 1856 remained the basis for regulation of American diplomatic personnel.

In the era after Adams and McLane the American diplomatic establishment both at home—in the Department of State in

Washington—and abroad—in the consulates and legations—declined markedly. The innovators, such as the first-rate secretaries of state, and the excellent envoys, such as Franklin and Jefferson in Paris or John Adams in London, were succeeded by rascals, scalawags, and blusterers abroad. In large part it was America's good fortune to be distant from European conflicts and interests. Had the nation been more central to the concerns of the great powers, the insolent pride, the supercilious confidence, with which Americans addressed the older and sometimes more powerful states of the world would surely have brought disaster. The old problems continued, but with the addition of degenerating political leadership and ethics. Secretary of State Martin Van Buren was among the first individuals in President Andrew Jackson's administration to apply the egalitarian ethics of the spoilsman. John Adams' steadfast refusal to appoint relatives to positions in the department gave way to an era in which not just secretaries of state but many federal officials appointed cousins, uncles, brothers, sons. If Washington society seemed one big happy family at times, it was no wonder. The distinction of formulating the spoilsman's credo for all of American politics, diplomatic appointments and domestic jobs alike, belonged to Secretary of State William L. Marcy, whose comment "To the victor belongs the spoils" became a cardinal principle of political behavior.

The militia diplomats of the revolutionary era had not always been diplomatic in demeanor and address, but most of them had been more circumspect than their successors, the political appointees, the "shirt-sleeve" officials of the nineteenth century. John Adams had angered Vergennes by boldness and confidence; Americans of later years became notable for much more offensive conduct. In perhaps the most remarkable such instance a secretary of state who should have known better, Daniel Webster, with unforgivable effrontery addressed a note to the Hapsburg emperor in the so-called Hülsemann affair of 1852. Webster was rejecting Austrian protests about American sympathy for the Hungarian rebellion of mid-century, and to the Austrian chargé, the Chevalier Hülsemann, he remarked, among other things, that "The power of this republic at the present time is spread over a region one of the richest and most fertile of the globe, and of an extent in comparison with which the possessions of the House of Hapsburg are but as a patch on the earth's surface." [8] The unhappy arrogance of the Ostend Manifesto two years later likewise characterized an era in which Americans possessed more confidence than sense, more luck than foresight. The signers of that undiplomatic document, among them a future President of the United States, James Buchanan, declared that if Spain did not accept their offer of a fair price for Cuba, "then by every law human and divine we shall be justified in wresting it from Spain." [9]

Not merely the spoils system, and perhaps the natural bumptiousness of Americans during the nineteenth century, but the pressures of the crusade against southern slavery made mediocrity in foreign relations difficult to resist. The emergence of a new political party in 1854, and the victory of the party in the national elections in 1860, encouraged supporters of Republicanism to hope for and expect immediate reward. Washington in 1861 swarmed with aspirants to office. Lincoln's secretary of state, William H. Seward, found a curious solution to the press of office seekers: He appointed his son as assistant secretary and turned the importunate business over to him after applying one simple test to current employees of the department. He asked each employee whether he was loyal to the Union or favored secession; those who admitted the latter sentiment were promptly discharged. Petitioners for positions thus vacated had to contend with Frederick Seward, who according to his father encountered the "whole array of friends seeking office—a hundred taking tickets where only one can draw a prize." [10]

During the Civil War it was not, of course, merely the Sewards, William and Frederick, operating in the Department of State in Washington, who lowered the quality of American foreign relations by introducing dozens of political appointees. The President himself, Abraham Lincoln, beset by the enormous crisis, used every device he could find to ease his task of preserving the Union. To his quick mind the possibility arose of dumping inconvenient politicians into the diplomatic or consular services. In the weeks between his election and inauguration Lincoln was accustomed to carry with him a little red book, and as he journeyed about the town of Springfield he was seen occasionally taking out the book to inscribe the name of someone or other. The book listed American legations and consulates and the President-elect wrote the names opposite the respective places. The more inconvenient a politician the farther away, geographically speaking, Lincoln was likely to place his reward.

This infusion of Republican talent into the machinery of American foreign relations at home and abroad led to deplorable results. During the Civil War the foreign relations of the republic sometimes appeared at their worst.

Cassius Marcellus Clay (no relation to his namesake of the sports world in the twentieth century) was a deserving politico from the border state of Kentucky, and Lincoln and Seward wanted to reward him with an appointment both impressive and remote. They sent him to Russia. Perhaps they also sensed that his peculiar personal qualities might raise the prestige of the United States in St. Petersburg, a capital not always noted for the height of its civilization. Appointed minister in 1862, Clay greatly impressed the Russians with his supply of bowie knives, great and serviceable weapons of which he had several varieties, including a pearl-handled pair for formal dress. Clay delighted in infuriating Russian noblemen to the point of duel, and since they invariably challenged, he had the choice of weapon. Just as invariably, he chose the bowie knife. Had the Russians known more of his background they would have indulged him more and challenged him less. Clay had survived a rough political career in Kentucky and was a tough fellow indeed. On one occasion his political enemies had imported an assassin from Natchez, the meanest town on the Mississippi. When the hired killer challenged Clay and fired point-blank at him, the shot struck the sheath of the great knife slung around Clay's neck and glanced off, whereupon Clay drew the knife, cut off one of the thug's ears, gouged out an eye, and threw him over a wall into a pond. Perhaps in Clay's instance there was something to be said for sending abroad diplomats who, if they did not possess experience in foreign affairs, nevertheless commanded respect in other departments of human relations.

After the high jinks of spoilsmen, of vote-counting secretaries and envoys, and of specially talented Civil War diplomats, it was no wonder that Seward's successor, Hamilton Fish, attempted to regenerate the department, restore morale, and put people to work. He faced a formidable task. Staff reductions—Congress in 1870 cut the staff from forty-eight to thirty-one—could have devastated the morale of a department which with justification could have felt persecuted, or at least out of favor, for another reason: The department in 1865 had been forced to move from its rambling quarters in a Georgian-style building near the Treasury into the austere and undiplomatic Washington Orphan Asylum, a graceless building set down in a then remote area of the city far out on Seventeenth Street. It must have been difficult to feel confident of one's future or of the value of diplomatic work when housed in an orphanage. Employees of the department doubtless greeted the completion of the initial wing of the new State, War, and Navy building in 1875 with something more than ordinary enthusiasm. However graceless the Victorian pilasters and mansards of the present-day executive offices of the President now appear, a century ago they would have seemed the height of Washingtonian luxury, and especially so when Fish led his little band of diplomatic assistants from the orphanage into the new building.

Despite lack of experience in foreign affairs, Fish in other ways contributed notably to the conduct of his department. He initiated one more in the series of department reorganizations that throughout the century had improved the institution. With a sternness that would have done credit to his predecessor J. Q. Adams, he began by lengthening business hours, setting them as 9:30 A.M. to 4:00 P.M., or longer if business required. He forbade employees to smoke anywhere in the new building (although one suspects he was unable to prevent some of them from chewing, as among the ornaments of the building that were preserved well into the twentieth century—the department moved its offices out of the building in 1947—were the big brass spittoons that were to be seen in every convenient corner of halls and offices; perhaps, of course, they were there for the convenience of visitors). He prohibited the reception of personal visits during working hours. Fish also experimented with the bureau organization created by McLane by adding agencies to handle such things as translations and telegraph services (the department's first telegrapher was appointed in 1867). He secured appointment of a third assistant secretary (a second had been appointed in 1866). Most important was his creation of a central file for papers of the department and his decision to classify and bind the department's miscellaneous correspondence. For those contributions historians have been grateful indeed.

But Fish could not destroy the vestiges of the old order, as the experiences of the next secretary, William M. Evarts, showed. Even before Rutherford B. Hayes took office as President in 1877, members of the forthcoming administration, including secretary-designate Evarts, had agreed on rules to protect the jobs of employees and perpetuate sound organization. Evarts nonetheless found the press of office seekers almost inescapable. Someone estimated there were more than seven thousand people attempting to win appointment to vacant consular posts, which prompted the witty Evarts to suggest that his office door be superscribed on the outside "Come ye Disconsulate" and on the inside "Abandon hope all ye who enter here."

3| Elitism and Reform

The period from the tenure of Fish and Evarts to the turn of the century was filled with the signs of changing times, some modest, like the introduction of the typewriter and carbon paper, some momentous, like the growing importance of the United States in world trade and politics. These changes, and not just the miserable performance of "common men" or spoilsmen in foreign affairs, required alterations in the organization for American diplomacy. The times of great national opportunity down the ages were followed by times of great national emergency, such as the first and second World Wars, times that called forth the talents of extraordinary men and foreshadowed the even more extraordinary destiny of the American nation. By a law of political gravitation as inexorable as any of those laws that seemed to require steady American expansion toward greatness, the American nation was drawn to involvement in world economic and political affairs.

But the *fin-de-siècle* produced a new problem in the organization of American foreign relations: elitism. Fearful of loss or defeat in foreign affairs, uncertain what there was to gain, Americans had long relegated diplomatic business to low importance in national affairs whenever the absence of external crisis or threat made that possible. In an almost uneventful late nineteenth century (uneventful in terms of American foreign relations), Americans had been content to continue past inattentions and congressional economies. The Department of State remained small, the pay of diplomatic secretaries and ministers low, the quality of representation inadequate. Because general public disinterest continued, because the diplomatic establishment remained small, and because government pay was hardly ever enough to meet the costs of life abroad as an American diplomat, the diplomatic service was susceptible to elitism. Increasing ties with British manners, style, and families (by virtue of the remarkable number of transatlantic marriages near the end of the century) came together with the revival of high international society following a rather graceless mid-century of political revolution and social tedium. This novel circumstance attracted into the service cultivated, well-educated young men acclimated to the transatlantic culture of the turn of the century, some of them even familiar with Europe by virtue of graduate study at a great German university or perhaps a postgraduate *Reisejahr*.

What a time of exuberance it was in the high society of the gay nineties, the height of the age of entrepreneurship, of great fortunes in the making, of unparalleled privilege! No wonder that some individuals who entered the diplomatic service in these times long afterward remembered them as a golden age. One American envoy later recalled that time of privilege and unlimited ambition, a time in which naïveté and sophistication mingled to produce the peculiar temperament of the era. The son of a shipping magnate, Lloyd C. Griscom had grown up with his own and his father's friends, one of whom had a house so hung with Italian paintings that one could not even go to the bathroom without making five or six masterpieces rattle. As his father's son, young Griscom could walk into any telegraph office, compose as long a message as he wished, sign it, and walk out. He could send freight anywhere without charge, board any steamship and travel to any point in the world, or take a train cross-country, all without paying a penny. "I can still remember my humiliation," he wrote, "when, obeying an Interstate Commerce Commission ruling, for the first time I had to stand at the window and buy a ticket like everybody else." [11]

Like many turn-of-the-century American envoys, Griscom had grown up in a society that had money to spend, that entertained noblemen and statesmen of foreign countries, traveled frequently and widely, savored rare brandies, and wielded absolute power within businesses, households, and families. Strict in discipline, full of advice and precept, the fathers of that Victorian age compensated for sternness with generosity. As a lad, Griscom could always get a dollar from his father, usually along with some maxim or adage, such as "Never give three poor reasons. Give a good one and stick to it." Such generosity apparently was essential to Victorian discipline, and of great importance in shaping the expectations of young men in the era, not always for the best as an anecdote of the day showed. A certain Mr. Dolan called his four sons into conference to explain that they were spending his fortune faster than he could make it and to ask them to consider what should be done about the situation. After an hour's discussion his sons returned and said: "Father, we've considered your predicament from every angle, and it's quite true something must be done. As far as we can see there's only one solution—you'll have to work at night."

In and around the houses of such families, the great and near great of the time visited and talked. Griscom and friends met Cecil Spring Rice, the first secretary of the British legation in Washington who later became the "Springy" of Theodore Roosevelt's "tennis cabinet." They sat at the table of Henry Adams, whose erudite, witty discourse and jaded cynicism captivated them. And although they attended the best schools of the Eastern seaboard, they strove less diligently than they might have, contenting themselves with a "gentleman's C," avoiding competition for attainment or learning (in some circles it was almost worse to get a "B" or, God forbid, an "A" than to receive a "D"). Students teased their tutors with impertinent impunity, copied feverishly from textbooks in unproctored examinations at the university, and sometimes received their exam papers unread but marked excellent.

Following graduation from college, the young gentlemen of the 1890s would make the grand tour of the Continent to round out their education, and with a letter of introduction to the American minister in London or Paris go off to be shown a bit of "diplomatic life." And in some such experience many young men found their calling, their motive for entering diplomatic service. The first diplomatic reception in a European capital presented a splendor likely to remain with an impressionable young man for years, perhaps life.

> The light from the great chandeliers flashed on the diamond tiaras of the women. Enormous jewels winked from the turbans of Indian princes clad in red, blue and yellow silks, and draped in ropes of pearls. I had never seen such dazzling attire—Austro-Hungarians in fabulous fur capes, Russians of the Imperial Guard in snowy white, military attachés in their regimentals, a Negro from Santo Domingo swathed in gold lace, white shirt bosoms slashed with ribbons—emerald, claret, burgundy, and occasionally the azure of the Garter.[12]

The real labors of diplomacy, the modest style and rank of American ministers abroad—in that same London mentioned above the American minister ranked below the envoys from Siam and Haiti and, as Griscom noticed, conducted business from a few rooms located in a cheap rent district—all were eclipsed in the fantastical grandeur of diplomatic society. The urbanity and wit of Secretary of State John Hay at the turn of the century, the social standing and literary turn of mind and phrase of Ambassador Joseph H. Choate in London, the invitations that came naturally to the hangers-on at the fringes of government affairs, especially those who had matriculated at Harvard, Yale, or Princeton, offset any natural hesitation of a young man entering work in which he had no guaranteed future, not even a sure job for more than a presidential administration.

There was something to be said for this elitism. The new American social diplomats were not simply imitating the British custom of younger sons going into the Foreign Office for a year or two at the end of formal schooling. As in other patterns in American foreign affairs, modest imitation was alloyed with distinctly American motives. The rapidly expanding diplomatic horizon after the Spanish-American War of 1898 required the United States to increase the number of overseas representatives. The continuing low pay of diplomatic officers as well as the costly requirements of the social climate of the era contributed much to a state of affairs in which a large proportion of diplomatic secretaries came from similar backgrounds, possessed similar education, social standing, and means. Many American diplomats actually began their careers by working without compensation. Congress ordinarily did not provide funds for ministers' private secretaries, and young men with independent incomes were drafted, willingly to be sure, to accompany diplomatic representatives in a sort of unpaid apprenticeship. With an allowance from a generous Victorian father, the income from personally-owned shares of stock or from part-ownership in a family concern, the young novices of the American diplomatic establishment sought experience at their own expense, counting themselves well repaid if they saw court life and high society, met the illustrious figures of the age, and at a later date received appointment as second or third secretary in one of the larger legations. In these beginning unpaid positions the "old boy" network of family and education became important, for there was no formal process by which one could apply for a job as private secretary to a new minister. One's family, friends, schoolmates, teachers, all moving in that same society, discovered openings and casually recommended or arranged for positions, perhaps over brandy and cigars at the end of one of the magnificent Philadelphia repasts at which a new minister or an official of the State Department might have been present.

And so in the conduct of American foreign relations there arose an elite corps of envoys—a development that would have been unimaginable to the shirt-sleeved representatives of earlier years or the renowned commissioners and ministers of the revolutionary era. It was, as mentioned, a perfectly understandable development. There was natural reinforcement to the elitist tendencies of a group that was from the outset select, men from the best families and schools. Reinforcement also came from the long-standing public indifference to and ignorance of American foreign affairs, an attitude often shared by Congress, which permitted diplomatic officers to maintain almost exclusive acquaintance with the business of state. Moreover, and without being secretive, American diplomatic officers often tended to be protective of their knowledge and experience. Certainly they were protective of their status. By the time serious reform of America's apparatus for foreign relations began to get under way early in the twentieth century, the elitism of the diplomatic corps lacked only two features: legislative protection for appointments and ensurance that people of wrong background or personality did not enter. The members of the diplomatic elite hence moved carefully, once the time was right, to obtain the proper legal protection for their privileges and perquisites, which they took to be necessarily synonymous with the best possible management of American foreign relations.

As the evidences of a new era were appearing, discussion arose of a reorganization of representation overseas. The most pressing need was for creation of a professional group with a close relation to the department at home, a single corps for consuls and diplomatic secretaries, so that easy transition from the consular to diplomatic work would increase the attractiveness of careers. Consular work, involving mostly the protection of American citizens in their travel and commerce abroad, and diplomatic work, involving the political relations among states, had been separated in American practice as in international usage and law. A consul could not easily become a diplomat, and diplomats refused to sully their hands with anything that hinted of consular work, except when they tried to correct abuses in their posts. This virtually ensured that the consular service would attract men of lesser ability. The history of American consular appointments seemed to bear out that generalization, especially in the years in which consuls had lived not from salary but from the collection of fees for performing duties on behalf of American citizens.

Much impetus for reform of overseas representation came from a man who, curiously, had risen to control of the consular service without traveling abroad to serve in or to inspect the consulates or, for that matter, simply to see what foreign countries looked like. Wilbur J. Carr had worked his way up from a clerkship in the department in Washington. He loved the problems of budget and personnel, and in long years of attention to such matters in the department had become acquainted with senators and congressmen. He used this acquaintance to advantage, promoting his dreams of a professional service. Laboring on Capitol Hill he made friends for reform by his quiet manner and obvious sincerity, and by the modesty of his budget requests, though some observers said that his modest requests hardly reflected the department's needs.

Concurrently some improvements occurred in American diplomatic organization. From 1895 onward individual congressmen had sought regularly to create a foreign service based on competitive examination and promotion on merit. Although the bills failed year after year, they had called attention to the need for reform. In his second administration President Grover Cleveland in 1895 by executive order required admission to lower diplomatic ranks by examination. Admittedly he did nothing to alter the political selection of higher ranking officers nor was his examination system entirely satisfactory. The weakness of the arrangement—dependent on presidential order—showed up when President William McKinley replaced 238 out of 272 consuls between March 4,

1897, and November 1, 1898. Still, Cleveland's executive order had been a beginning.

More progress had occurred when Elihu Root succeeded Hay as secretary in 1905. Root was a conservative lawyer. Curiously, he was much better at devising organizational plans than he was at administration. There is an old story, perhaps apocryphal, of Root's idea of perfection: himself doing all the work of the department, while all the other members stood around him in admiring awe. But before coming to the State Department he had reorganized the War Department, so miserable in performance during the Spanish-American War; he was largely responsible for creation of the general staff system. In his tenure at State, he applied his talent for rationalization and divided the department into sections with regional responsibilities. A combination of regional divisions and functional bureaus has remained the basis of State Department organization down to the present day.

Another important improvement came under Theodore Roosevelt in 1906 when Secretary Root collaborated with Senator Henry Cabot Lodge to propose new legislation that would establish grades in the consular service and apply civil service principles to the selection and promotion of consular officers and proposed the establishment of an inspection system for consular posts. The bill emerged from Congress without the provision concerning selection and promotion. Roosevelt then issued an executive order providing rules like those in the original bill, and thereafter the consular service was administered on a nonpartisan merit basis. It was perhaps only a minor inconsistency that TR could sponsor reform in the consular service, while he made capricious appointments to the diplomatic service. The diplomatic career of young Joseph C. Grew began shortly after the turn of the century when TR heard about a brave chap who had crawled into a cave in China and shot a tiger. "By Jove," said the President, "I'll have to do something for that young man." As good as his word, he appointed Grew third secretary of the embassy in Mexico City.

Changes once begun were difficult to stop. Although President William Howard Taft followed TR's lead in regularizing the careers of consuls, he too overlooked the diplomatic service. And a troubling lack of permanence remained in the arrangement of change through executive orders. With the Cleveland-McKinley example in mind it was difficult to feel confident that change would last. Many individuals in the State Department and Congress believed in a merit system for both the diplomatic and consular services, one set out by legislation. Businessmen too were increasingly sensitive to the need for more efficient representation. Wilbur Carr became a frequent visitor to Congress and appeared time and again as the department's spokesman in hearings for proposed legislation. He had learned of the weight congressmen would attach to expressions of public opinion and buttressed his arguments with exhibits of letters and newspaper editorials, among which were impressive, even urgent calls for the kind of representation that could serve the needs of citizens of a nation engaged in the struggle for survival against citizens and subjects of other governments.

Partly because of Carr's influence, partly because the time for change was overdue, the years immediately after the World War of 1914–1918 began to fill with discussion over organizational reform. The war itself had contributed to desire for action, for deficiencies in diplomatic reporting on the eve of the war, the confusion into which the continuation of the war had thrown consular officers and affairs, the occasional sheer inability to carry on diplomatic business—all were reminders that something had to be done.

An additional reason for change was the obvious incompetence or at least unsuitability of some of President Woodrow Wilson's appointees, who had become centers of controversy, defended and vilified with equal passion for their insight/dullness, ability/incompetence during the years of neutrality and war. In truth, for all of Wilson's morality and despite his Progressive principles, he was vulnerable to criticism in the matter of diplomatic appointments. He could not stand some of his own appointees and deplored their work. Perhaps the most controversial of his choices had been Walter Hines Page, the New York publisher sent to the Court of St. James's, who became a notorious Anglophile. Page's attitudes served to focus postwar argument over whether the United States should have entered the war and in whose interests and for whose benefit entry had occurred. Wilson had dismissed much of what Page wrote, and relied, instead, on Colonel Edward M. House for difficult wartime diplomacy. But there had been other lapses. The President had permitted a partisan turnabout in diplomatic posts. Congressman John Jacob Rogers of Massachusetts calculated that only four of the forty-one ambassadors and ministers who had served under President Taft survived; and of the first fifty-one individuals Wilson appointed to diplomatic missions, only two had possessed diplomatic experience. It was true that some of the Wilson appointees, Page among others, were men of considerable personal attainment, including high intelligence and undoubted patriotism. Still, with a Tammany judge, a police court lawyer, and other amateurs among the throng of new envoys, the appointees generally were undistinguished, to say the least.

The demands for reform thus increased notably. Beginning in 1919, Congressman Rogers annually introduced bills "for the improvement of the foreign service." By 1924 the advocates of "reorganization and improvement of the foreign service" were mounting an irresistible campaign for amalgamation of the diplomatic and consular services, for increased salaries, for retirement benefits and representation allowances, all of which propositions appeared in Rogers' bill of that year. Proponents of reform pointed to the necessity of having the best possible organization of foreign affairs. Carr, ever ready to testify, had been saying for more than a decade that

> the United States has completely changed its position in international affairs and it is never going to be less important but is probably going to exceed our wildest dreams in the importance of its relation to world affairs in the future. That being so, we need the very best, the very strongest, machinery that we can get to protect our interests abroad. Our commerce is growing by leaps and bounds. Our investments are reaching all parts of the earth; our business men are going everywhere; our contacts are becoming more inti-

mate and more numerous, and as the process goes on it inevitably follows that the chances for conflict of interest, for misunderstanding, for infringement upon our rights are going to be greatly multiplied. . . . So we ought to have the most competent men we can find in every place in which we are represented to protect our interests, to resist encroachments upon our rights, to further our commerce, and to protect our citizens, and prevent misunderstanding of our motives.[13]

Somewhat surprisingly, and certainly so to the well-to-do young men in the diplomatic service (and to their older friends who had entered the service at the turn of the century), demands for reform began to turn against the elite itself. One of the notable results of the World War had been to bring foreign affairs to the attention of broad masses of the American people, to many persons who earlier had given them little or no attention. These individuals began to see that the diplomatic service had become almost the preserve of the young and older rich with their interlocking connections of birth, education, and friendship. No longer, they vowed, would this arrangement continue. Everything had seemed set up to keep out the bright and competent, in favor of the wellborn, mannered, wealthy members of the elite. Salaries in the diplomatic service were inadequate; although the United States government had not, as had the British, required young entrants to possess independent means, in practice only those with private income could enter. It had become the custom in the department to discourage young men who would have no income beyond their salaries. In a standard reply to inquiries about the necessity of private income for diplomatic secretaries the department was using a bureaucratic circumlocution that even members of Congress found remarkable. It had been repeated so often that one of the assistant secretaries of state knew it by heart and quoted it in testimony on the Rogers bill of 1924:

> The experience of the department is that at present the remuneration of secretaries in the diplomatic service is unfortunately not such as to enable the department to assure them that they will be able to live on their salaries at all posts to which they might be sent.[14]

The supporters of the elite apparently had done everything to preserve their dominance in the diplomatic service. There was of course no retirement plan. Department officers told Congress about members of the consular and diplomatic services who had left government work after ten or fifteen years because they had to begin thinking about providing for their families in old age, men in their prime of age and experience whom the department could hardly afford to lose. With experience as consuls or as secretaries in legations or embassies they could take employment with some bank or commercial enterprise at two or three times their former salaries or even larger increases. One consul who had earned a little more than $7,000 a year accepted employment at an annual salary in excess of $20,000. Another had left a post where he had earned $4,500 to become president of a bank at more than $50,000 a year.

Every passing day put the United States government at greater disadvantage, for other nations of the world, great and small, had reacted to the deficiencies in their diplomatic structures exposed by the Great War and there had been a flood of reforms. Britain, France, Norway, Sweden, the Netherlands, Italy—these were only a few of the countries that had undertaken improvement of their diplomatic services, and many had adopted reforms almost precisely similar to those proposed by Congressman Rogers, albeit with salaries and allowances even more generous. In 1924 discontented members of the State Department—not members of the elite, of course—openly admired the new dictator of Italy, Benito Mussolini, not so much because he made the Italian trains run on time, as Americans would later note, but because he had combined the Italian diplomatic and consular services, raised salaries and allowances, and provided for a probationary period for new officers in which their suitability could be confirmed in practice.

About this time it was noted that the American diplomatic and consular services were short of personnel and could not attract enough individuals of intelligence and capability to meet the needs. In congressional hearings department officers related the instance of a diplomatic secretary posted to London who requested a year's leave to hunt lions in Africa. Refused permission, he threatened to quit, and because there was no man to replace him the department gave in rather than lose his future services. Moreover, many consular and diplomatic officers could not be discharged because no better men were available among members of the diplomatic service. A young member of the diplomatic service testified before a committee in 1924 that

> you hear very frequently about the boys with the white spats, the tea drinkers, the cookie pushers, and while they are a very small minority, they make a noise entirely disproportionate to their numbers. Any cranks, and any sort of freaks, make an impression that is out of proportion to their numbers. But they are a reproach to us. . . . Our great problem now is to attract enough men so that we will have a real choice of material and crowd out those incompetents and defectives. If we can do that we can build up the service, but until we can do that we can not hope to do it.[15]

Impressed, the chairman of the House Committee on Foreign Affairs remarked that

> two or three men of the type you mention will discredit a whole nation.
> MR. GIBSON: There is no doubt of it.
> THE CHAIRMAN: As a rule they do not do much work.
> MR. GIBSON: We have some of the type who do not do any work.
> THE CHAIRMAN: As a rule they are men of independent influence and therefore feel that they are more or less free from governmental control.
> MR. GIBSON: And they are so long as we can not get men from whom to choose. . . . It makes it hard to have a very effective discipline if you can not replace a man when he should be put out of the service.[16]

Perhaps nothing impressed Congress in 1924 so much as a demonstration of the dearth of young men interested in diplomatic careers. In the preceding year approximately three thousand persons had written the department inquiring about positions abroad. Only forty-five had applied to take the written and oral examinations. Some were immediately disqualified because admission was limited by considerations of geographical distribution and other requirements. Thirty-six men took the exams. Eleven passed both tests. The department thus had to accept and appoint virtually anyone who could meet the minimum qualifications of the examinations. In the period from 1919 to 1922, eighty-three persons had passed the exams, and seventy had been appointed. One congressman asked Third Assistant Secretary of State J. Butler Wright: "Of those that took the examinations, how many of them were either boneheads or absurd?" Wright answered without hesitation: "I should say, roughly, 33⅓ %." [17]

There followed the passage of the Rogers Act of May 24, 1924, the most notable legislation ever to affect the organization of American foreign relations. It at last put diplomatic representation on a formal basis. It combined the two services, diplomatic and consular, into a single Foreign Service, with entry at the bottom by competitive examination and promotion on merit. The new service was ranked to provide for orderly promotion all the way to the highest levels, those of career minister or career ambassador. Salaries were increased, though not to levels comparable to those of British and Italian envoys. A contributory retirement fund was established, which also provided benefits for disabled officers— that is, if disability was not due to "vicious habits, intemperance, or willful misconduct." [18] The Rogers Act contained two important additional points: Inferior men currently in consular or diplomatic posts abroad were to be weeded out, and personnel were to rotate from overseas posts to Washington assignments, not in an invariable alternation but frequently enough so that consular and diplomatic officers could stay in touch with developments at home and also gain experience in the administrative bureaus of the department.

The result was a momentous transformation in the work of the department at home and of the representatives abroad. Morale soared, the quality of men and of work improved, and the Foreign Service rapidly increased in size and professional skill. American diplomacy became both a career and a profession. Men with long service accumulated in the years before they had acquired legislative protection soon were filling more of the intermediate and higher posts in the department in Washington. The era had passed when a change in presidential administration would sweep out the assistant secretaries and bureau chiefs and as many underlings as the incoming politicos could get their hands on; destruction of a good department, as had happened at the beginning of the Garfield-Arthur Administration in 1881 and the McKinley Administration in 1897, became a thing of the past. If a new President did feel it necessary to replace officers in key posts, he could find many of the men he would need within the career service, ready for a tour of duty in Washington. In subsequent years an experienced group of men became heads of bureaus and assistant secretaries, positions with operational responsibility. Unlike earlier groups of promising men, almost always the product of happenstance, the new group contained such men as Hugh Gibson, William Phillips, and Joseph Grew, a professional fraternity that for the first time could enable the State Department to carry on the foreign relations of a great nation.

The Rogers Act carefully organized the diplomatic establishment, and not a moment too soon. For in less than a generation the interests and actions of the United States in world affairs—commercial, financial, political, strategic—were to increase beyond the wildest dreams of 1924 to a size and complexity far more extensive than Congressman Rogers or Wilbur Carr or anyone else of their time could have anticipated.

CHAPTER TWO

Refining the Organization: Since 1924

The Rogers Act brought American foreign relations into the modern age but not into an era free of problems. Professionalization of the Foreign Service solved some difficulties. No longer were American envoys laughingstocks, fit subjects for the humor and scorn of Europeans. Although some Americans appointed to high places abroad were chosen for political reasons, they often were intelligent and tactful and did well for their country, and those appointees who were incompetent were backed up by professional Foreign Service men and women (almost from the outset, women began to enter the service). Even so, the times were out of joint, and problems arose incessantly that even the best-trained envoys and staffs could not have hoped to solve easily or perhaps even with the utmost effort. For a few brief years after passage of the Rogers Act the countries and peoples of the world sailed serenely on a summer sea. With the beginning of the Great Depression the problems of American foreign relations increased dramatically. World War II was fought in a coalition, which required a continuance of diplomacy, some of it of a very complicated sort; and there were many neutrals, which likewise required attention. Then shortly after the war, from 1946 to 1948, American leaders at last decided to take up the responsibilities of world power, and a new age of diplomacy and foreign policy opened that has continued to the present time—an era that has involved extraordinary diplomatic efforts, the almost constant concern for American fortunes not merely in the large and important countries but, more recently, in the smaller and hitherto unimportant. In this new era the work of the Foreign Service, and of the Department of State in Washington, has passed from complexity to complexity. The task of organizing for what the next day or week will bring has proved never-ending. Americans thus discovered that the Rogers Act was only a beginning of the business of improving the organization.

1| Weaknesses of the Rogers Act

Perhaps the most notable characteristic of foreign representation during the first half century after the Rogers Act was the continuation of the custom, which had become a tradition, of political appointments. There seemed no real way to remove political appointments from the conduct of American foreign relations.[1]

The career people always felt resentment toward political appointments. At the change of an administration or the whim of a highly placed Washingtonian they might have to surrender their hard-won embassy or legation to, perhaps, a kazoo manufacturer from Peoria. Often, though, the gaffes of amateurs amused the professionals almost enough to offset some of their irritation, as when one appointee had all his embassy stationery stamped "Barker Bakes Better Biscuits." For the edification of the embassy's neighbors this same individual each morning played the American national anthem over an amplified outdoor sound system.

Admittedly there has been justification for a modest number of political appointments to high-level diplomatic positions. Many men of attainment have never been Foreign Service officers. It would be capricious to bar individuals from diplomatic service because they had not made diplomacy their careers. Indeed, some of these men, not careerists, have become virtual professionals because of the many assignments they have undertaken—Chester Bowles, ambassador to India, under secretary of state, in earlier years a congressman and earlier still an official of the wartime Office of Price Administration, or W. Averell Harriman, David K. E. Bruce, and Ellsworth Bunker, who have had much to offer the nation.

Another perspective on political appointments has appeared in the comments of an ambassador who evidently had become sensitive to criticism. "The phrase political appointee is misleading," he wrote. "What is meant is that the President selects a person of proven abilities who has been successful in his particular field. Such men have had much experience and can often be more effective than career men in particular situations . . . the most essential qualification in an Ambassador, is good judgment and the courage to act on that judgment. A career officer with equally good judgment is intimidated by his awareness that in service life . . . it is more advantageous . . . to maintain . . . an acceptable attitude." [2] Or as a State Department task force reported in 1970, ". . . conformity is prized in the Foreign Service above all other qualities." [3]

The continuation of political appointments after the Rogers Act was partly related to considerations of purse. Some of the most important diplomatic capitals and traditional listening posts in the Western world have also been places in which diplomatic society flourished, where entertainment was extensive and expensive and the need for presence most acute. Even though many Foreign Service officers could supplement their salaries, few could afford the huge amounts called for in London, Paris, Rome, or others of the European capitals. Congress after World War I did not provide anything approaching an adequate representation or post allowance. American career diplomats in expensive capitals could not be expected to spend the tens of thousand of dollars annually, sometimes hundreds of thousands. They have had to ask for transfer from such posts, where the costs of representation drove them near to or into bankruptcy. When G. Frederick Reinhardt appeared before the Senate some years ago in a hearing on his confirmation as ambassador to Rome, one of the most expensive posts, Senator Hickenlooper asked him how he intended to bear the anticipated costs. Reinhardt cautiously answered that he hoped Congress would be generous and appropriate additional money. "Hope," replied Hickenlooper drily, "springs eternal."

Far less defensible has been the way in which private fortunes have been used not to meet costs of representation but to secure diplomatic appointment for individuals who possess no desire to serve the country but seek to satisfy a whim, or social ambition, or as one American appointee frankly admitted, because his psychiatrist recommended that he go abroad for a while. Years ago an able diplomat had deplored the "snobbishness that leads grown-up Americans to seek appointment as minister or ambassador to gratify their desire to shine in the society of European courts. The fact that this is often done to satisfy the social ambition of their wives doesn't make it any better." [4]

The tales—all of them true or close to the truth—of ineptitude in American diplomatic appointments for political reasons, most of them related to campaign contributions, are legion. One such case concerned Maxwell H. Gluck, designated by the Eisenhower Administration as ambassador to Ceylon. In the course of his confirmation Gluck admitted to the Foreign Relations Committee that he did not know the name of the country's prime minister. He had contributed $21,500 to the 1956 Republican national campaign, and his nomination was not withdrawn. He took a short time to learn a little more about his prospective post, then returned to be confirmed. "Gluck," he said waggishly, "it rhymes with luck." Lucky Gluck and his wife set a gay social pace in Ceylon, and after little more than a year returned to the United States and Gluck's clothing business, but not before Mrs. Gluck had sold her excess clothing at public auction in Colombo, a gaffe so offensive that the Ceylonese government apparently considered lodging a protest.

Less well-known but equally inappropriate was President Lyndon B. Johnson's nomination of a Virginia horse breeder and gentleman, Raymond R. Guest, as ambassador to Ireland. Guest, in contrast to Gluck, knew the names of Irish leaders but revealed a different gap in his preparation. After most of the Senate committee members had professed no particular interest in questioning him, Senator George D. Aiken of Vermont took over:

> I might ask one question. Are you familiar with the Irish political situation?
> MR. GUEST. Yes, sir.
> SENATOR AIKEN. Do you know what part Ireland plays in NATO?
> MR. GUEST. Well, I know that they have played a very big peace-keeping role.
> SENATOR AIKEN. They do not belong to NATO.
> MR. GUEST. I beg your pardon, sir. I thought you said U.N. I beg your pardon.
> SENATOR AIKEN. That is all right.[5]

Despite investigations and increasing resistance in the Department of State and the Senate, the road to an ambassadorship via a political contribution has remained open a half century after the Rogers Act. Only the cost of advancement has changed. A newspaper editorial concerned with the "auction" of diplomatic posts after the 1972 presidential election revealed some extraordinary statistics. Mrs. Ruth L. Farkas of New York, of the Alexander's department store family, was appointed ambassador to Luxembourg after contributing $300,000 to President Nixon's reelection campaign; and she did it on the easy-payment plan because she did not give two-thirds of the money until after her candidate had been reelected. That same year the ambassador to El Salvador managed to obtain his embassy because he had contributed nearly $40,000 to the Republican Party in the four years preceding his appointment. By 1972 some of the more desirable posts in the Western Hemisphere were costing almost as much as their European counterparts. The representative to Jamaica and his father-in-law together contributed about a quarter of a million dollars to the GOP between 1968 and 1972. As *The New York Times* remarked, "At first glance, that seems like an awful lot, but then Jamaica really is a gem of an isle." [6]

Somehow, despite the depressing features of so many hearings on diplomatic appointments, the Foreign Relations Committee has kept its sense of humor year after weary year. Most of the monied nominees have received confirmation; rarely has one aroused so much antagonism that he was denied appointment. Franklin D. Roosevelt once nominated Ed Flynn, political boss of the Bronx, to be ambassador to Australia, a nomination he had to withdraw when the Senate rose up in indignation, but such instances have been unusual. Confirmation hearings for the most part reflected a friendly atmosphere in which even embarrassing disclosures of ignorance or personal ambition could be overlooked. Occasionally there was a bit of humor on display, as in the confirmation of Chester Bowles as ambassador to India. Senator Fulbright inquired of Bowles, a Democrat, whether he had been a Republican in earlier days.

MR. BOWLES. I was brought up a very good Republican.

SENATOR FULBRIGHT. When did you become a Democrat?

MR. BOWLES. I started arguing with my father about the League of Nations as a very young man . . . I thought he had rather narrow ideas, and when I was in school we had very violent arguments on the League . . . and I think that drove me into the Democratic tradition. . . .

SENATOR FULBRIGHT. I was rather interested. My father was a Republican too.

MR. BOWLES. We are both of good sound stock.

SENATOR SMITH (of New Jersey). It is pathetic to hear all this evidence of a fall from grace.

SENATOR SPARKMAN. May I add that my mother's father was a Republican?

SENATOR GILLETTE. And may I add that both my father and mother were Republicans?

SENATOR FULBRIGHT. That just shows a man shouldn't give up hope. People do learn.[7]

The least humor and the most choler appeared in confirmation hearings when the Senate was in the hands of the opposition party, when a committee with a Democratic majority considered a Republican nominated by a Republican President or vice versa. Such feelings came to the surface in the hearings on Mrs. Clare

Booth Luce's nomination as ambassador to Brazil in 1959, a year in which the nonpartisan period in Eisenhower's presidency had about run its course. Fulbright, as chairman of the committee, was at his best as he tangled with Mrs. Luce. At issue were the lady's several intemperate statements as a party politician during the 1940s, a lonely if not lone Republican adrift in, as it had seemed to her, a Democratic sea. Fulbright read out: "For 20 years mortal enemies of ours have been growing and thriving in the organism of the Democratic Party. There is only one way to dislodge them. We must shake them all out. Yes, the tree of government must be shaken hard. Then these rotten apples, these mortal enemies, will fall out before all from the top branches." Mrs. Luce pertly remarked that that was pretty good oratory, then squirmed under Fulbright's query as to whether she had been referring to President Truman. She finally admitted she had not meant to include Truman even by implication. Fulbright reminded her of another statement in which she had referred to Franklin D. Roosevelt as the "only American President who ever lied us into a war, because he did not have the political courage to lead us into it." [8] A reminder that she had called Truman the handpicked candidate of the big-city political bosses alienated several committee members, lifelong Democrats, who believed her judgment and language too intemperate to permit confirmation, no matter how well she had served the Eisenhower Administration as ambassador to Italy. In a curious denouement Mrs. Luce received confirmation by an overwhelming vote, then resigned before taking up her duties in Rio, but not before remarking that one of her senatorial antagonists seemed to have been kicked in the head by a horse.

2| Foreign Service Self-Defense

From the outset, of course, the Rogers Act had given evidence of being flawed—for it naturally could not resolve every single problem of American diplomatic organization. It had provided job security and instituted a system of competitive examination and promotion on merit, which would enhance the quality and prospects of diplomats. It certainly could not prevent political appointments; that was a tradition not subject to an act of Congress. And the act struck ineffectively at several aspects of the elitism that had increased in the service in recent decades. The elite had not been a group based on ability, but on birth, social agility, connection, wealth, and education. The frank intent of the act had been to make a diplomatic career attractive to men from more varied backgrounds, without independent means and social connections. The social and educational similarity of American diplomatic officers had earned unfavorable comment. Still, the act could not make elitism disappear. The simple truth was that the Ivy League colleges and universities dominated American higher education in the 1920s and would do so for at least another decade, and hence most of the applicants for the new Foreign Service turned out to be from the same elite backgrounds that had so bothered the supporters of Congressman Rogers. Moreover, it was impossible to rid the service—and probably undesirable, too, for they were good men—of the individuals who had been in the upper reaches of the old diplomatic service, and so they continued to dominate the new appointments. The written examination was only half of the total examination for entrance into the Foreign Service. The other half was the oral exam, and here the old tycoons of the State Department or tycoon-like officers home on leave would ask the right questions to get the right answers (if they approved of a young man or woman) or, if necessary, ask the wrong questions and get the right answers.

The inadequacies of the Rogers Act, together with the enormous multiplication of chores in the making of American foreign policy and the carrying out of American foreign relations, inspired several notable efforts to change the organization of the Department of State and the Foreign Service. The first of these, coming just after the end of World War II, proved a defense of the Foreign Service against further liberalization. And it came just in time. Immediately after the war there arose a direct challenge to the idea of a separate Foreign Service. The Bureau of the

Budget, at the request of Secretary of State James F. Brynes for advice on yet another reorganization of the department, remarked that the government had long passed the time when a closed elite corps was the only alternative to patronage. The bureau concluded that it would be wiser to amalgamate the department's civil servants and Foreign Service officers, a recommendation that stimulated the Foreign Service to lobbying in Congress. Despite opposition within the State Department, reservations from other cabinet departments such as Agriculture and Labor, which had substantial interests and personnel involved overseas, and a near veto from the White House, the Foreign Service Act of 1946 passed, and it possessed just the conservative character for which Foreign Service officers had hoped. After "honest reexamination" of the service, the House Committee on Foreign Affairs had sponsored a bill that reaffirmed the concept that professional service should remain paramount and endorsed entry at the bottom by competitive examination, esprit de corps, adequate salaries and allowances, and internal administration. There was also the principle of "promotion up or selection out." (More about this latter point shortly.) The most important change brought by the act of 1946 pertained to the training—the formal training—of diplomats, a novelty signalized by the creation of the Foreign Service Institute.

The reason for formal training was apparently an accommodation to criticism. Actually, training programs strengthened the claim of the Foreign Service to a special competence in federal service. Critics of the Foreign Service and of American foreign relations had long considered on-the-job training unworthy of professional work. Diplomacy seemed to need the aura or veneer, not to say preparation, of formal training. In the years following Pearl Harbor, American foreign relations undoubtedly had taken on complexity and urgency. With life-or-death issues of national and international affairs, prudence required more effort to ensure that diplomats would be ready for their labors. The cold war encouraged people inside and outside the service who argued that it should become more like the military services, at least in respect to the new Foreign Service Institute. The institute promised to end attempts to model the diplomatic service after the castes of the army and navy, with their distinctive academies for production of trained, professional career officers.

In truth, the training program designed in 1946 has had serious and continuing deficiencies. It never came close to the expectations that attended its founding. Diplomats today begin their careers with a bare five weeks of "basic training" at the Foreign Service Institute. In those weeks a bewildering series of subjects receive brief, and one suspects confused, attention. The newly appointed probationary junior officer confronts in week-long units the department's organization, the other agencies involved in American foreign affairs, introductory "management considerations," and problems of Foreign Service life. In the fifth week he receives instruction and practice in observing, reporting, and negotiating; his final week is spent as an intern in one of the department offices related to his first overseas assignment.

The syllabus for the basic course for Foreign Service officers admits limited intentions, so perhaps it is no wonder that results are limited. The institute does not "attempt to *train,* but simply to *introduce* . . . the broad range of activities which constitute modern diplomacy and to provide some of the background. . . . Specific training for future assignments will come later." [9] How the novice in diplomacy must look to that promise! Fresh from some American university campus or brief association with a corporation he faces the traditions and hierarchies and stratified social orders and ordinances of government on the one hand and diplomatic society on the other. Fulfillment of that promise is long in coming, if it ever does. The diplomatic novice is likely to go overseas with little more than that course of instruction, to learn his position—perhaps his craft—on the job, the way American diplomats always have. If he is lucky he will have learned enough about government forms and formalities and about starting a peripatetic life to make it.

Some new Foreign Service probationers receive slightly more extensive training before taking up duties at an overseas post, depending on the career specialization they choose. There are four such specializations, or cones as they are called in the service: political, economic, administrative, and consular. Officers who elect careers as consuls study for eighteen days the laws and regulations governing procedure in the major fields of consular activity. Here the extent of government paperwork is revealed, and it is a wonder that new officers do not flee the service, or at least the consular cone. After eighteen days of training, including two days of "advanced consular studies" in which foreign trade and commerce, foreign exchange programs, narcotics and management are briskly dispatched, the young consul embarks for distant places, certificate of competence in hand. The serious and eager junior consul, once at his post, will begin the department's eighteen-month correspondence course on consular affairs, there to discover the substance of all the laws, regulations, and procedures whose titles he vaguely remembers having heard about in his whirlwind training. Similarly, administrative cone officers receive brief special instruction. Political and economic officers may attend a two-week area studies course to introduce them to the region of their first assignment, an intellectual version of the well-known tourist tour—Western Europe in two weeks, or "it's Tuesday, so it must be Belgium."

Perhaps the most extensive formal training goes to officers who decide to specialize in economic affairs. If their early work is good and if they are fortunate, they may after a time receive assignment to the Foreign Service's Economic/Commercial Studies Course, twenty-six weeks of "intensive and comprehensive . . . economic training . . . the equivalent of a strong undergraduate major in economics with additional professional instruction in commercial subjects." [10] The program was expanded to its present form in July 1970, after the secretary of state had called for professional training to make Foreign Service officers more responsive to the needs of American business abroad.

For economists, and for a few promising political and administrative officers, the department holds out the further possibility of graduate training at a prominent American university at department expense. Foreign Service officers of promise may receive assignment to enroll in an MA program in international relations or in the MBA program at Harvard Business School to learn management or international economics. Such assignments do not fall to every officer, or even to a large proportion. The rest have to depend on what they can pick up from their superiors and from colleagues in the two or three years between first assignments and "commissioning" in the Foreign Service, usually after the officer has been promoted three times, reaching the FSO-5 rank and the end of probation.

One of the many self-study task forces appointed in the Department of State concluded recently that at the end of probation officers need three or four months of training in "core skills and management techniques particularly relevant to the profession," and that officers whose experience had "concentrated in a functional cone abroad" need a better understanding of "the roles of the Service and the Department in formulating and executing foreign policy." [11] Typically for the service's and the department's approaches to training, people recognized the good idea and turned it into a bad idea. The proposed three-to-four-month instruction "proved to be impracticable," though the institute hoped that "the three-week course to be offered will essentially meet the objectives" of the three-to-four-month course originally recommended. Newly commissioned officers spend a week studying the roles of the department and other foreign affairs agencies in policy, including the role of Congress and "operational concepts of the Foreign Service personnel system," along with another negotiation simulation. In the second week they move to a unified communications course in which participants "strive to improve their skills—speaking, listening, reading and writing." In the third and final week of the course the institute introduces officers to an executive studies seminar, emphasizing "self-development, motivation and goal orientation, how to exert influence, and other management instruction of utility." [12]

There are other educational possibilities for Foreign Service officers. At times in their careers, officers attend language schools, depending on aptitudes and assignments, and as they reach and pass mid-career they may attend the ten-month senior seminar or shorter seminars on "relevant" topics. Topical seminars in recent years have lasted anywhere from two days to three weeks, and addressed such topics as "The New Left: An International Overview," "Radical Ideologies and Political Systems," "Computers and Foreign Affairs," and "Theories of International Relations" (in four days!). The seminars may well have reached their acme in one on "Intelligence and Foreign Affairs," all sessions of which were classified. Attending officers were not permitted to carry any notes outside the classrooms. How much use such a seminar is to a man who attends only to return to his remote post was an unanswered question. The impression of absurdity grows when one realizes that assigned readings for the "classified seminar" come from well-publicized, widely available published literature.

Only the highest ranking officers, the chiefs of mission and counselors of embassy or deputy chiefs of mission, will have opportunity to prepare extensively for assignments. Upon appointment to a position a new ambassador will receive several weeks of briefing, perhaps as many as six, from department officers who carry on most of the business with that country from Washington. Sometimes less senior officers will sit in. For political appointees to ambassadorial or ministerial rank or to administrative positions, the briefing includes sessions on government operations, department procedures and policies, and embassy security. Charles Frankel was at first annoyed, then amazed, and finally amused by the air of confidentiality that surrounded his briefing on security, which consisted in large part of vague discussion of electronic listening devices fully described in current press and periodical stories. His briefing officer proved unable to give him definitions of security classifications, and after boasting that he —and only a few others—knew everything, but everything, about Frankel, was nonplussed to learn that Frankel had worked in naval intelligence during the war. John Kenneth Galbraith noted that a diplomatic or security briefing consisted "in approximately equal parts of what one already knows, couldn't remember or doesn't entirely believe." His briefings summarized, he wrote, amounted to strongly suggested discretion. "Silence is advised for the first six months to be followed by a policy of silence." The stolidity represented in such briefings undoubtedly had some part in bringing Galbraith to remark a few months later that Secretary of State Dean Rusk was a traditionalist who thought that "because foreign policy was bad under Truman and bad under Eisenhower it should be at least mediocre under Kennedy." [13]

The instructional programs set out here do not add up to much training, at least not by standards in other professions. Henry A. Kissinger has properly criticized this rapid preparation: "State Department training is in the direction of reporting and negotiation, not of thinking in terms of national policy. They are trained to give a very good account of what somebody said to them. They can give a much less good account of what this means." [14] Comparison with the training of representatives of foreign governments, especially Soviet diplomats, presents stark contrast. As Westerners who have dealt with them testify, Soviet diplomats are trained in international law, in minute knowledge of treaties in force between the Soviet Union and the country to which they are sent; they are linguistically qualified for foreign assignment and seasoned in the Foreign Ministry in Moscow before they ever set foot in a mission, all of which makes them not only competent but formidable negotiators.

With so much to criticize in training there again appeared suggestions for producing diplomats like the military academies turned out officers, even the thought of creating a new one- or two-year graduate school. The latter suggestion provoked irate reactions from diplomats who considered even short-term training for diplomacy as another of the assaults on their tradition of innate capability, intuition, and experience. Ellis Briggs harrumphed his disdain for a "National Foreign Affairs College on the Graduate Level, a mastodon postgraduate supermarket with ivory towers manned by hot-and-cold running professors." [15] And to some people, the idea of such an academy for diplomats promised not a supply of emissaries but an assembly-line monopolized for producing robots, each like the others.

3| Expansion, Bureaucracy, Management

It was one thing to respond to the new needs of American foreign relations by instituting all sorts of training programs, hoping thereby to retain the traditional esprit of the Foreign Service. The fact remained that the service was too chummy and clubby a group, too friendly to those within its precincts; and the group was also far too small to face the multiplying problems of American foreign relations in the years after World War II. A whole series of changes therefore looked to a livening up and, of course, an enlarging of the service.

The Foreign Service Act of 1946 announced the principle of "promotion up or selection out." It was a remarkable principle. After time in grade, if one had not been "selected" for promotion he would be "selected out" or, in plain language, fired. The act did not fix the permissible time in grade for Foreign Service ranks but left that to the secretary of state.

It was a principle long overdue. Between the wars the Foreign Service's power to set and administer standards for entry and promotion meant that the old-boy network became formal, though disguised. Senior men in the service created by the Rogers Act had entered soon after the turn of the century. A few other Brahmin types had come along and been admitted. In practice the legislation of 1924 permitted a kind of closed situation in which Joseph C. Grew, Hugh Gibson, and others gave each other the good jobs and encouraged younger officers who had the right backgrounds—Ivy League, social connections, money. The tycoons were in a position to limit the mobility of consular officers who wished to transfer to diplomatic assignments. As senior officers of the Foreign Service, diplomats of the old school thus had ability to reinforce, reward, and preserve the style and mannerisms of American diplomacy.

The situation needed to be changed, but the act of 1946,

despite the best of intentions, did not do the job. Whether a result of confusion in the new postwar era of expansion in personnel, policy, and relations or of softness of heart, the selection-out principle did not receive vigorous application. Officers ranked in the bottom 5 percent of the service on the basis of performance and other characteristics (personality, appearance, propriety, wife's culinary ability and social grace) were to be selected out each year and replaced by new entrants at the bottom of the service. Actually, far fewer than 5 percent of the service were discharged in any year. Selection out became a joke. The service by 1954 had cast out only an average of sixteen men per year.[16]

And so it happened that as "promotion up or selection out" was failing, a new move was made to bring in a great mass of competent individuals through what in department jargon was known as "lateral entry." [17] In a more attractive piece of department jargon this became known as "Wristonization." When the Republican Party took over the federal government in 1953, Secretary of State John Foster Dulles appointed a Public Committee on Personnel. In short order the committee, under the direction of Henry M. Wriston, president of Brown University, called for a larger service, with broader recruitment, more specialized officers, improved training, and easier provision for lateral entry. In some respects the committee's recommendations were really just restatements of earlier proposals or directives that the department, especially the Foreign Service, had managed to avoid fulfilling. The suggestions were no more acceptable from the Wriston committee, but because there was a threat of more reforms in consequence of parallel study being done in the White House and elsewhere, the Foreign Service and the department now hastened to do what Wriston told them. Such a course seemed preferable to having the career service amalgamated into the federal civil service, whence it would disappear forever into the bureaucratic jumble.

The Wriston committee recommended "integration" directly into the middle ranks of the Foreign Service of individuals who occupied positions in Washington that required domestic and foreign experience. Some Foreign Service staff members also were to enter the Foreign Service. This integration, coupled with expanded recruitment for bottom-entry positions, caused the size of the Foreign Service to triple in the three years following the committee's report, with enormous long-range effects. Wristonization ensured that in the next decade and a half the Foreign Service would become superannuated, with almost as many officers over forty-five years of age as under, and more than twice as many officers in the top four as in the bottom four ranks. Many of the Wriston-era lateral entrants got the top positions. In 1962 lateral entrants comprised a third of all ambassadors (other than political appointees) and two-thirds of deputy chiefs of mission. This trend apparently decreased in subsequent years.

After 1954, with the new people swelling the ranks, the days seemed gone of a small service, homogeneous, with entry only at the bottom and advancement only on merit and experience. Knowledge that worse things could have come did not dispel the gloom of veteran officers. Ambassador Ellis Briggs recalled at his retirement that there had been "only thirteen American ambassadors in the world when I entered the Foreign Service in 1925. Each ambassador was serving in a country that possessed power as well as sovereignty—a country, that is, of importance to the United States." [18] It was not the end of the world, but it was the end of a tradition.

In retrospect it seems clear that in the years since the close of World War II each decade has seen its attempted solutions to the department's organization problems. The first was the principle of "promotion up or selection out," announced in 1946. The second was Wristonization, set out in 1954 and 1955. The third, which had no formal announcement but came gradually into vogue during the 1960s, was the idea of management.

Wristonization, with its large additions of personnel to the Foreign Service, had inaugurated an era in which the difficulties of operating a large scale diplomatic establishment would lead naturally to applications of the management techniques employed in other large organizations. On every hand the size of American

foreign and domestic diplomatic operations increased. Had the
postwar personnel increases been confined to Washington, they
would have been bad enough, but increases were not so confined,
and the scale of American representation overseas increased enormously. At Prague shortly after the war a new American ambassador found a mission of about eighty persons, which he considered far too many. After he had tried everything he could think
of, without succeeding in having any of his staff recalled, his
communist hosts solved the problem of overstaffing when they
declared five-sixths of the embassy staff *persona non grata* and
gave them a bare forty-eight hours to leave Czechoslovakia.

It would never again be so easy to solve the problem of being
"overstaffed, overstuffed, and overstymied." Galbraith arrived in
India early in the Kennedy Administration to find a mission of
more than three hundred persons. (He was probably not surprised,
or at least not dismayed, at anything he found. He characterized
the department as "simply too large . . . there are more people
on C Street than there are problems.") [19] About five years later,
the new American ambassador to Brazil discovered that 920
Americans made up the mission, an overgrowth threatening to
have undiplomatic consequences as Brazilians virtually stumbled
over an American adviser or supervisor every time they turned
around in Rio. That figure, 920 Americans, did not include the
510 Peace Corpsmen or the 1,000 Brazilians who worked in the
embassy. About this same time Kissinger was writing that the diplomatic establishment was "so overstaffed that it makes thinking
impossible," with individuals abroad filing endless reports with
the result that "no senior official can possibly read everything that
comes in." [20] Nor was Kissinger alone in disapproval of proliferation. One of the earlier ambassadors to Brazil had resisted the
assignment of a science attaché, cabling that the embassy needed
a science attaché "the way a cigar-store Indian needs a bras-
siere." [21] The telegram did not provoke mirth in Washington, and
more to the point it did not prevent assignment of the attaché.
Ultimately there were *two* science attachés in Rio.

Ambassador John W. Tuthill made history as a manager and

as a hatchet man when he cut the mission in Rio by 32 percent in what he called "Operation Topsy," because of the way the mission had "jest growed and growed." He attributed his success in an endeavor at which many an old hand had failed to modern management principles. Brazil, he wrote, "represented an almost perfect example of the lack of management policy in government operations abroad." [22] Almost lost in the approbation of such management triumphs was the realization that the Inspectorate General could not have been doing its job when such conditions had developed.

Perhaps inevitably, there was some early confusion over just what management was, and how it applied to the problems of diplomacy. It was easy to confuse management with administration, something that had always been a part of diplomatic work. Technically, administration and management differed. Administration constituted the "low level support" organization for political, economic, and consular work of the Foreign Service—supply, bookkeeping, and the other services necessary for diplomatic activity such as budgets, payrolls, assignments and promotions, communications and couriers, and the Foreign Service Institute. Management comprised more than personnel administration or bookkeeping. The miracles of management included Planning, Programming, and Budgeting along with contingency planning and data processing. In the Kennedy years McNamara's "whiz kids" in Defense had generated considerable envy among their distant cousins in State with their insouciant confidence, jargon, clicking and humming computers, and most of all with their success in budget battles on Capitol Hill. Finally State had no choice. The performance of the Defense Department had been so impressive, at least outwardly, that in 1966 President Lyndon B. Johnson ordered every government agency to develop a Planning, Programming, and Budgeting System. Unfortunately, the prospects that such a system would work in foreign policy and affairs were poor.[23]

Diplomats of the old school, and some of the new, did not find it easy to become managers; they made mistakes even when they began to move in some of the "right" directions. State did not acquire its first computer until 1962, and then used it for payrolls and personnel records. Not until mid-decade did the department's Record Services Division inaugurate a data-document storage and retrieval system.

But gradually the first confusions cleared up and the new imperatives, such as the need for specialization of diplomatic officers, became apparent to almost everyone. Time was when a diplomat, like the Renaissance gentleman, had to be well-rounded, ready to take on varied international work in his country's service. Indeed, in American experience dating from the Rogers Act diplomats were even supposed to master and perform consular duties, though in law and tradition these had been no part of a diplomat's work. In the management age that "jack-of-all-trades" approach to diplomatic work quickly became passé, as adoption of a career tracking system, the cone system, showed. The generalists in diplomacy were gone in the postwar years, their passage confirmed when a department self-study spoke of the need for "foreign affairs executives."

Regrettably for American foreign relations, proponents of scientific management in the department exaggerated its promise. Some department and service members, many of them in middle and senior positions, succumbed to the implications of management science and soon were overgeneralizing from personnel to policy. From the rarefied atmosphere of the sixth and seventh floors of the department, or from the top floor of one of the luxurious new embassies constructed abroad to dramatize American presence, it became easy at first, and then habitual, to believe that problems of foreign relations were merely extensions of the personnel problems that had dominated departmental, presidential, and congressional concerns since the war. If only we could use our men correctly, so the rationale went, problems of policy and relations would be manageable, perhaps even eradicated. "Official personnel policy," one experienced diplomat wrote recently, "is to 'locate' prospective managers of foreign affairs and to bring them along to 'manage.' The implication is that management ability is easily transferable, without loss, regardless of what it is applied to. The Harvard Business School may have lost some confidence in this notion, but the State Department has not. In the Department's view, the foreign country, the problem, the technology, the economics, are all grist for the manager's mill; he can get what information he needs from 'experts,' he and only he can then apply the magic touch of 'management skill'; and, hey presto, everything will work satisfactorily." [24] There has indeed been reason to fear that a pool of managers for program direction positions would gradually replace diplomatic generalists, whereupon that superior being would disappear from the Foreign Service as trends to ease the rigor of entering examinations proceeded to their natural consequences.

It was especially easy to believe the promises of management at a time when American academic enthusiasm for the new principles were so high. Political scientists in the 1960s were turning to quantitative and model-building studies of policy and government structure. Many academic types found their ways onto the staffs of commissions, where with "a number of useful ideas to offer, but no broad familiarity with foreign policy or the diplomatic traditions they sought to change, they made the mistake of tying themselves to a military-ideological conception of world affairs. They were essentially technocrats. Modern management, social science, and military technology, the perceptions of a McNamara, a Rostow, and a Taylor were to be applied wholesale to an 'anachronistic' tradition of interstate relations. Instead of slimming down an inefficient bureaucracy, their goal was to expand its size, make its structure more complex, and make its functions more mechanistic." [25] Worse, they tended to accept bureaucratic failings—infighting, fragmentation, immense size—as unalterable, proposing that wisdom lay in understanding the *status quo,* comprehending the laws of bureaucracy and adjusting one's own behavior.

The new faith in management aroused some skepticism at the outset, especially among diplomats who had romantic attachments to the idea of the diplomat as a generalist, or who had experience which prevented belief that problems of policy and relations could be managed, whether personnel problems or not. As people took sides on management, they almost seemed to be showing a generation gap. It annoyed diplomats, some of them at high rank after decades of service, to be told by young management wizards that they had been doing their job all wrong. It was irritating, not just for experienced diplomats but for younger officers, to see the faster rate at which new administrators received promotions. There was humor and bitterness in Briggs' wry observation that even the official definition of the attributes of high diplomatic officers had come to reflect the age of the bureaucrat and manager. The new criteria for career minister, as he noted, required that the candidate "will have demonstrated complete awareness of the new dimensions of diplomacy in the 1960s, in both the substantive and management-administrative fields." [26]

"Management equals diplomacy." That assumption of the new age of the 1960s called forth vituperative debate. Personnel specialists, career evaluators, ministers of embassy for administrative affairs—all amounted (so said the critics of management) to no more than "glorified janitors, supply clerks, and pants pressers." What the department needed, said the same critic, was a new type of diplomat, a bureaucrat exterminator.[27]

One special managerial prescription, contingency planning, quickly raised difficulties. When Walt W. Rostow became chairman of State's Policy Planning Staff in 1961 he learned to his surprise that the department did not have formal statements of policy defining and informing its efforts in all areas and countries. Any competent manager could see immediately that this was a grievous deficiency. Rostow directed that such planning papers be prepared, and that they contain statements of long- and short-range objectives as well as recommended courses of action. Like military contingency plans, they were to be updated. Said one diplomat, a young one, who quit in disgust: "If the Rostow effort had been taken seriously (which it was not), the time of the bureaucracy would have been devoted in large part to the continual writing, negotiating, and rewriting of these 'plans.' . . . nothing could seem more ridiculous . . . to spend most of the government's time on planning is to escape reality." As former Assistant Secretary Frankel wrote, "No matter how much sound study goes into the long-range reports, they are shots in the dark." [28]

It made sense to anticipate opponents and the course of events but less sense to plan for every contingency or to plan for any contingency in detail. One could not just cut out contingency plans or policies and hang them out to dry. Decisions would have to take account of circumstances. All too often the latter differed from the prospects. All depended once again on the intuition and judgment of a man matured by experience and by his experience prepared for general responsibility. In a hypothetical but characteristic anecdote, an American diplomat forecast what he thought would be the failure of postwar American plans to deal broadly with problems of reconstruction and maintaining peace. General George C. Marshall as secretary of state, he said, "will summon his aides and ask what is the most compelling problem facing the American people. Having identified the problem, he will demand the formulation of a plan, and in due course a plan will be adopted. Let us call it Operation World Savior. And just as in those vast enterprises during the war, the resources of the United States government and its allies will be mobilized to promote that operation. Diplomats will be deployed like task forces, and Foreign Ministers will do setting-up exercises. Finally the great moment arrives. The Secretary of State, having secured—so he thinks—the last contingency between Antwerp and Zanzibar, presses the button that puts Operation World Savior in motion. Mankind, unanimous at last, is supposed to march forward. And what happens then? . . . Nothing happens! San Marino and Monte Carlo say the hell with it. Operation World Saviour is a shambles." [29]

In perhaps the saddest consequence of the new management emphasis, a management-labor dichotomy emerged in the department and especially the Foreign Service. The old unified service, with its camaraderie, gave way to a larger, more impersonal organization in which the interests of lower- and middle-level officers no longer seemed to coincide with those of senior officers, so that officers did not trust the normal selection and promotion system. In recent years the Foreign Service has had to establish a process for the grievances of officers who suspect or allege unfair treatment. It has had to permit officers to see the greater portion of the fitness reports written about them by their superiors and used by boards for evaluation of officers. Institution of such procedures says much about what has happened—a shift from emphasis on the profession and toward emphasis on the career. And the procedures have not been especially useful to aggrieved officers. John D. Hemenway, selected out after remaining too long in grade, appealed his case. After three years of hearings and delays, a review board found him justified in complaint, recommended that he be reinstated in the Foreign Service and awarded back pay for the years of unwarranted suspension. But higher officers in the Foreign Service simply refused to accept and carry out the review board's recommendations, which left Hemenway no recourse except petition to Congress. Indeed, Hemenway became a familiar figure in the hearing rooms of the Foreign Relations Committee where he appeared from time to time to re-argue his case and to "testify" on the appointments to various positions of high officers in the State Department who had failed to see him vindicated. But to no avail. Hemenway has not been reinstated.[30]

How, then, does one "tune up" a large group of people to meet the increasing demands of American foreign relations during the past half century? The department and the Foreign Service have continued to face the problems of improving the organization. There is continuing competition as individuals, men and women, try to better their positions as they work presumably for the betterment of their country's foreign relations. Opportunities unfortunately vary from group to group. Managers compete with department bureaucrats. Members of missions abroad compete with each other. The consuls continue to compete with the diplomatic secretaries. The terms of competition are sometimes obscured by vestiges of "class consciousness," of snobbish attitudes left over from the older days or re-created by young snobs.

Most important, the relation of the Foreign Service to the department, or its role within the department and in American foreign affairs, still lacks definition after all the efforts. Perhaps the only point on which people agree in this respect is that the Foreign Service is more than a group of employees available for overseas duty. Some officers believe the Foreign Service is the heart or the backbone or some other vital part of the department's anatomy. In another metaphor popular in Washington the service is the "cutting edge" of the department or, as President Kennedy put it, the point of the spear. For Henry Villard it is the "link that connects international events with Washington." [31] Some officers emphasize the service's special responsibility to contribute to policy, whether the President and his associates want it or not, and others stress the service's work in foreign relations, regardless of contributions to policy. For an outsider it is disconcerting to hear one ranking officer pronounce that the Foreign Service is the department, while another down the corridor, as exalted in position, declares the department and the service are, and of right ought to be, distinct and separate. (It is clear that they are separate, but not equal. The service is still an elite.) The department works for the secretary of state, some officers say, whereas the Foreign Service is responsible only to the President, for (to revert to anatomical imagery) the service is his right arm in the making of policy.

All these formulas and impressionistic, sometimes almost bombastic, assertions of the relations and duties of the parts of the foreign affairs establishment bespeak the confusion of that establishment. But perhaps there is hope. How else should order emerge, than out of confusion?

CHAPTER THREE

Making Foreign Policy

In the course of World War II the State Department encountered more subtle and more serious problems than personnel difficulties and organizational adjustments. During the war the department lost much influence over policy, most of it to representatives of the military, a trend that continued in subsequent years. This development did much to shape American foreign relations in the cold war and the Vietnam decade.

Nearly everyone agrees that State lost influence to the military, although not everyone agrees on how and why, or on the consequences. In the 1970s, as Americans hope for a generation of peace and look back over a generation of conflict, that shift of influence away from the diplomats and to the warriors looms as the course of much that seems to have gone wrong with American foreign affairs in an era of nationalist revolutions around the world. In an age obsessed with the power of the military-industrial complex, a time when moral objections to the use of force are increasing (in a poll in May 1974 more than two-thirds of American college students opposed the use of force even in a just cause), after massive applications of coercion have failed to fulfill even limited national objectives as in Vietnam, the influence of the military on foreign policy has caused widespread anxiety. Has the republic veered from its earlier, purer, democratic commitment to responsible, peaceful, non-Machiavellian diplomacy? Have brass hats and technocrats of the Pentagon and the "spooks" of the CIA usurped the constitutional functions of the secretary of state and his department?

1| State's Historic Role

Much unease over military influence in foreign policy derives from the pervasiveness of what one American diplomat has described as the myth of the Golden Age, the conviction that at some time in the past there was an era when the State Department worked harmoniously, productively, and with insight to the problems of foreign affairs, a time when it worked through the secretary of state to dispense weighty and sage advice to the President.[1] In fact, there never was such a golden age, at least not one that endured longer than a year or two at any given time.

The secretary of state's role as chief adviser on foreign policy has always been personal rather than constitutional or institutional. The Constitution, of course, implied but did not create cabinet offices. Those offices and the duties associated with them have developed as legislation and tradition augmented each other, often inconsistently. The first secretary of state, Thomas Jefferson, had to fight for every bit of influence he possessed in Washington's cabinet, and as often as he won in matters affecting foreign affairs he lost to Alexander Hamilton, the ambitious secretary of the treasury. According to the early practices of the American presidency, cabinet officers as a group were the principal advisers of the President, and individually were administrators of government departments. Since secretaries of state, like other cabinet officers, received appointment as often for political reasons as for ability, there was little to support the view that they should monopolize policy on matters pertaining to foreign affairs.

In sum, the influence of the secretary of state has always depended on his relations with the President and on his prestige or expertise in foreign affairs. Indeed, for many secretaries of state, good personal relations with the chief executive have depended from the first on recognition that advice would not be sought. In the United States strong Presidents characteristically have taken charge of the foreign policy of their administrations, some of them so completely that, like Presidents Woodrow Wilson and Franklin D. Roosevelt, they are said to have been their own secretaries of state. In the twentieth century the extent to which a President directs foreign affairs has become a measure of his forcefulness and vigor in office. From Theodore Roosevelt onward, world leadership has comprised an essential element of presidential stature, and one wonders whether a President can achieve greatness in the eyes of his countrymen and of historians by domestic accomplishment alone. Presidential direction of foreign affairs encourages a public ignorant of the work of professional diplomacy and of the Department of State to feel modest contempt for secretaries of state who allow themselves to be supplanted in policy making.

Since World War II, Americans have been conditioned by the likes of Dean Acheson and John Foster Dulles to expect a secretary of state to loom in the sea of international affairs like the Rock of Gibraltar, to speak with thunderous voice the implacable certainties of national interest and national destiny. But such men were exceptions, not types; few secretaries of state have risen to such preeminence, and still fewer Presidents have desired or tolerated secretaries who overshadowed them or who even challenged their personal control of foreign relations. Of the great secretaries of state in the twentieth century, not even a handful outshone their superiors. John Hay, who made most of his reputation as a diplomat under McKinley and earlier, was able to remain in office under Theodore Roosevelt only because he had cultural and literary interests and did not derive his whole satisfaction in life from his work as a diplomat; as Hay's health declined, TR hit his stride on the way to world power. Wilson deliberately appointed Robert Lansing secretary of state to succeed William Jennings Bryan because Lansing appeared to be a narrow-minded international lawyer, in Wilson's opinion no possible rival for leadership in foreign affairs. Charles Evans Hughes scored diplomatic triumphs but faded quickly from influence on foreign affairs. His successors, Frank B. Kellogg and Henry L. Stimson, overshadowed Presidents Calvin Coolidge and Herbert Hoover in spite of the self-restraint of American diplomatic doctrines at the time, with at least one contentious result: Hoover always felt that the Stimson Doctrine—the refusal to recognize changes in the Asian *status quo* that resulted from the use of force—was his idea and should have gone down in history as the Hoover Doctrine.

Even John F. Kennedy, that reinvigorator of so many high democratic ideals, intended to be his own secretary of state and appointed the reserved, cautious, unprepossessing Dean Rusk mainly as a caretaker for the department. William Rogers, Nixon's secretary of state, became an object of contempt when it appeared that he was pusillanimous in office, a figurehead, perhaps a custodian of creaky and outmoded diplomatic agencies, while Nixon and Henry Kissinger handled all the business of importance. Time and again in the press Rogers was characterized as a weak man and criticized for remaining in office while someone else controlled policy, as if his situation—his predicament—was unprecedented.

Paradoxically, phrase-making has been more attractive to Americans, by far, than any issue or concern over who was making the phrases. Americans have been less sensitive to the weaknesses of presidential diplomacy, less perceptive even than some foreign observers in whose eyes presidential initiatives have too often seemed bombastic and newsmaking, but without substance. "Certain monsters and freaks are scurrying hither and thither," the New China News Agency commented at the time of Lyndon B. Johnson's Christmas "Peace Offensive" of 1965–1966 during the great thirty-seven-day halt in the bombing of North Vietnam. "Typical Johnson razzle-dazzle" is the way one American diplomat has since described it.[2] Similarly, the production of headlines, and little else, appeared for Kennedy's Alliance for Progress and later for the Nixon-Kissinger Year of Europe and such a list could be much longer. A full compilation of mistaken, ill-timed, or ineffectual presidential pronunciamentos would include a multitude of entries less worthy of banner headlines but sadly demonstrative of the too-wide gap between those who make policy and those who possess familiarity with day-to-day conditions, problems, and prospects in the many countries and regions of the world.

2| State's Lost Influence and the Rise of the Military

It would be easy to beg the question as to why the State Department has suffered such a loss of influence in policy making in recent years, to say simply that the department has lost the trust of the chief executive or that it has never been all that powerful anyway. In general terms those answers would be valid, but they would forestall further inquiry into not just what was happening among the few individuals who occupied the Oval Office in one building and the office of the secretary in another, but how the institutions so laboriously constructed for American foreign relations were performing and in what ways they were proving inadequate or weak.

The style of Franklin Roosevelt's presidency, and some of his prejudices, greatly diminished the power of the diplomatic establishment, even before war came in 1941. Although it now seems that Secretary Cordell Hull maintained considerable influence over foreign policies and relations up to the outbreak of the European war, never during the 1930s did the State Department possess anything approaching control of American foreign relations. Roosevelt, indifferent to organizational traditions, was manipulative, impulsive, and freewheeling in administering the affairs of the nation. He reached out to persons closest to him for ideas, relied on friends for advice on policy, elevated some of them to high positions, such as Sumner Welles, whom he appointed undersecretary of state, and established out-of-channels relations with other appointees. Roosevelt had no particular interest in efficient organization, clarity of responsibilities, or avoidance of overlap, and displayed airy contempt toward professional diplomats, whom he considered too narrow. During the thirties the expansion of overseas interests and the operations of cabinet departments other than State—principally Commerce and Treasury—continued without hindrance.

When war came Roosevelt easily and naturally followed the implications of his style and attitudes and relied for advice on a circle of friends and confidants regardless of their official standing or lack of it. Early in the war, Hull and the State Department received clear indication that they were to be sidelined for the duration. Roosevelt relied on Harry Hopkins for the most important diplomatic missions—including one to Moscow in mid-1941 to anticipate Soviet-American partnership in war against Germany. Concurrently, the influence of Henry Morgenthau and his Treasury Department was increasing. Already in the middle thirties there had been instances in which Morgenthau and the Treasury Department had determined American relations with Germany and China to a far greater extent than had the State Department. The war's emergencies did nothing to reverse this relationship; instead, they augmented the importance of economic planning and management at home and in relations with allies, and ultimately, in the notorious Morgenthau Plan, in relations with the enemy.

Hull himself was partly to blame for his department's loss of influence. His personality, of course, tended to subtract from his importance. He was given to rages, which became sources of amusement in the department, and he lisped noticeably—a trait which, combined with a suitable rage, would make the corridor outside his office ring with secretarial shouts of "Jesus Cwitht!" But his major contribution to the department's downgrading was his foolish notion that he should distinguish between foreign policy and the operations incidental to foreign policy. The making of policy, he liked to believe, was the business of his cabinet department. The carrying out of policy, he fondly explained to himself and to anyone who cared to listen, might well occur outside his department. He willingly observed the creation and growth of so-called "operational" agencies, intelligence services such as the Office of Strategic Services, and other organizations devised in FDR's usual patchwork manner to handle any new problem or perhaps only a new facet of an old one. The result gradually became apparent: Late in the war the United States government had representatives from forty-four different agencies in London, all ostensibly carrying on the work of foreign relations in wartime. Small wonder that diplomats were drafted into the armed forces during the war, without objection by the secretary. It would have been difficult to prove that diplomacy—in the State Department at least—was an essential wartime occupation.

During the war, as the star of State dimmed, that of the military services grew brighter, and perhaps inevitably so. As one historian has observed, diplomacy and strategy often become one and the same thing during a war and require the intrusion of military officers into discussions and decisions that in peacetime might not be any of their concern.[3] The diplomats cooperated in the war years. After Pearl Harbor, disgusted, angry, and betrayed, Hull was ready to turn over dealings with the perfidious Japanese to the military so that they could administer appropriate punishment for misconduct in diplomatic relations. As the war progressed the military services were invited and even forced to make decisions of a political nature, so much so that Stimson as secretary of war and George Marshall as chief of staff frequently complained that they were acting in default of direction or decision from the State Department. The Joint State-War-Navy Coordinating Committee became the best known of several organizations in which military representatives came to share with diplomats the responsibility for policy in wartime, but in the work of this committee the two service departments dominated the State Department.

No better illustration of the importance of the power accruing to the military during the war can be found than in the planning and preparation for administration of occupied enemy territories when the war should have reached successful conclusion. Already in 1942, while the United States was still recovering from the deceitful destruction of the Pacific battleship fleet, the army was establishing schools to train military and civilian personnel as administrators for the areas it expected to wrest back from National Socialist and Japanese domination. The establishment of those schools reflected incredible optimism at such an early point in the war, when the promise of victory was yet remote; the coalition had barely formed, and the assault on German-held Europe was only a dream. But in the context of shifting responsibilities for policy, those schools represented a pattern: The military services planned ahead, and by planning, deciding, and doing, acquired political responsibilities. After the war, the military services did indeed preside over occupied enemy territories, and it was a long time before the diplomatic establishment recovered any influence in those areas.

So much for the war, one might say. It is easy to see how and why influence over foreign policy shifted during the emergency, but why did State thereafter not recover some of its influence? Why did the military retain so much influence?

The first reason why wartime relations continued into peacetime, and perhaps one of the most important, was that so many of the same men remained active in government and in positions of power. True, there were dramatic changes at the very top—Truman replacing FDR, Edward R. Stettinius succeeding Hull. But for the most part Truman depended on the same circle of advisers to whom FDR had turned. As for Stettinius, like Hull before him, he contributed to the wartime weakness of State in policy, at least in the view of Secretary of War Stimson who considered Stettinius pleasant and brisk but "unable to make his machine go," well-intentioned but "not very firm in his decisions and character, and the result is that we have been called in in several issues in which while we have some military interest, we are being made to take a very predominating part." [4]

Other wartime officials were, however, still at the center of affairs. General Marshall, and later General Dwight D. Eisenhower, succeeded to the foremost civil offices in the national government. There is little doubt that Truman turned to Marshall because the general could do what the diplomats could not—get information, make decisions, and get work done. Eisenhower's election to the presidency came because the people of the country thought that he, likewise, could get things done. Furthermore, he had a nice smile—for a general.

A second reason for the State Department's continued loss of influence in peacetime was the inability to look ahead and plan for the future. That deficiency was serious in a time of rapid change in international circumstances and national temperament, such as the early cold war years. Even under decisive, driving men like Acheson, the department proved incapable of a systematic approach to foreign affairs, an incapacity most conspicuous in the department's failure to institutionalize planning, which the military services, with their traditions of general staffs, contingency planning, and strategic and tactical studies, had long since achieved.

The importance of planning for the medium and long terms in foreign affairs was obvious to postwar diplomats. In 1947, the same year in which the military and intelligence services were reorganized and centralized, George C. Marshall created a Policy Planning Staff headed by George Kennan. The staff became almost mythically important in American foreign affairs of the postwar era but not because of its achievements. The idea had been good —let a dozen or so diplomats ruminate on world affairs and American foreign relations and try to devise proposals, goals, and plans, which the government should try to realize. Think big, think ahead—five, ten, or even fifteen years ahead. That was in 1947.

The department's inability to rise above the day-to-day press of diplomatic business resulted in a notable misuse of the Policy Planning Staff. By 1949, Acheson as secretary of state was bragging on Capitol Hill about his staff and the way they thought three, six, nine, and even twelve months (not years) into the future. Again and again those senior, experienced, and presumably wise diplomats necessarily turned their attention from the world of the future and from American policies and goals of the future back to the present, to the momentary crises of the cold war, to what was happening now. Perhaps in self-justification, diplomats developed a perverse pride in being men of the moment who could get things done each day, keep the paper moving from their desk to someone else's, make decisions and take action every day in the real world, rather than reflect on a future that might never come, or that would come in a form altogether different from that anticipated. As one senior department official wrote in the Johnson years:

> At the end of a day spent in making decisions . . . the official may well wonder why he should spend the evening reading the scholarly treatise on the future which arrived on his desk in the morning. Is long-term policy created by abstract theorizing about future goals? Or is it created out of the succession of immediate, practical decisions of the kind he has been making all day long? The life of the official does not merely turn him aside from more spacious reflections: it creates in him professional habits and a kind of professional pride which lead him to believe that reality is where the nitty-gritty is, that policy isn't made by the great thinkers but by the tough men who take each problem as it comes and do the best they can with it.[5]

A final consideration has diminished the influence of the State Department relative to that of the military services. One of the most astute students of American negotiating style, and of all that can be learned about a nation's diplomacy from such study, has concluded that the cold war was prolonged by a misconception in dealing with communist countries, which is at the same time the reason for the increase in influence of military men in policy. Americans have considered their communist adversaries, and often their other adversaries or even their allies, as being impervious to reason.[6]

The assumption grew out of the American experience of the thirties, one more facet of the now notorious Munich syndrome, which has inspired so much of American foreign policy (as well as the policy of other nations) since the war. There had come a time in the thirties when the Western democracies awoke, finally realizing that Hitler was not amenable to reason, that (to borrow a phrase from postwar melodramas) they could not go on meeting like this, as at Munich, conveying slices of territory and populations to a dictator already contemplating his next aggression. The leaders of Britain, France, and the United States finally knew that there was only one thing Hitler would understand, only one way in which they could put a stop to the expansion of National Socialism and its racial, moral, political, and economic systems. Jaw, jaw, jaw was no longer better than war. What Americans had learned dealing with Hitler they now applied to relations with the Soviet Union. Americans by 1944 were already speaking of the Russians in the same terms they had applied to the Germans and Japanese: as Americans saw it, Russians considered talk cheap and responded only to crude power and to determination to use it. According to one interpretation the Russians even became heirs to the hatred of Germans that had reached feverish intensity during World War II.

One of the last times American and Soviet diplomats found much to talk about was at the Yalta Conference. The dashing of hopes founded on such Yalta-signed documents as the Declaration on Liberated Europe confirmed the impression that the Soviets would be surly and aggressive after the war. The failure of the Baruch Plan to internationalize control of atomic energy, whatever the faults of American procedure and the justification for Soviet suspicions, provided another example of the futility of negotiating important issues with the Soviet regime.

In both theoretical and practical terms, communist intransigence decreased the area within which American diplomats worked and increased the province of the military. Time and again in the cold war, that new functional relation received demonstration. It would be exaggeration or distortion to say that it was always wrong to give so much weight to the views or solutions of military men. But negotiation is a process of give and take. In the era of zero-sum games, when ideological factors were overestimated, when the United States was willing to give little for the sake of improved relations, there was almost no diplomacy in the old sense.

And so the State Department lost out, during the war and in the postwar era. Looking inward to its personnel problems, bemoaning its disappearing influence and modest budget, the department and the Foreign Service found themselves tossed about in a sea of change, disoriented at the sight of unfamiliar landmarks, surprised by squalls, and finally washed up, the new State Department building lying like a great gray whale on the riverbanks in Washington away from the center of town—and of power—from there to watch the conception and execution of the integrated diplomatic-military policies of a new age.

3| Effects of Military Influence on Policy

Had Americans and Russians not become locked in struggle at the end of World War II, perhaps relations between diplomats and military men might have reverted to some approximation of prewar conditions. American diplomats might have returned to a genteel exchange of diplomatic notes and the assemblage of reports, and military men might have reverted to the modest excitements of war gaming and contingency planning, perhaps to find some delight in the novelties proffered by continued technical advance. The continuation of military men and wartime leaders in important positions, the inability of the State Department to rise above the routine and plan for the future, misconceptions about allies and adversaries—these would have exerted far less influence on the organization of policy making and the conduct of foreign relations than they did under cold war circumstances.

The conduct and goals of World War II had not prepared Americans to face the peculiar challenges of a cold war so soon after the end of a global conflict. Indeed, despite all accusations of cold war critics, Americans were much slower than their allies the British to recognize the new hostility, or at least discord, that would characterize Western relations with Russia. In the darkest days of World War II it was comforting to imagine that Wilsonian visions would at last come true, that through surpassing struggle, almost unbearable suffering, and supreme perseverence, a world at peace, a world free from war and threats of war, could arise like Phoenix. That dream found special development in America. Americans had a history in which the complicated factors of alliance politics, of continuing enmities and security problems, had never had much part. Americans little understood the cynicism with which the Russians pursued a postwar order that would ensure the security of the Soviet Union in the West.

It greatly surprised Americans that security problems were to outlive the destruction of National Socialism and Japanese militarism. Several years elapsed before America's leaders recovered sufficiently to institutionalize the ideas of men like Kennan, who finally set out the evolving assumptions on which both diplomatic and military elements of cold war policies would depend. Because security remained problematic after the war, the normal peacetime separation between diplomacy and strategy did not recur, so that national defense and national security remained entwined with foreign policy and foreign relations.

In the insecure years after World War II, Americans lacked confidence that diplomacy alone would adequately guard their interests, and so the policies and doctrines of the cold war were marked by integration of diplomatic and military elements. The most fundamental such policy, ironically, was the device of a long-time diplomat, George F. Kennan. In his famous X-article of July 1947, Kennan reiterated the conclusions he had expressed earlier, more privately, in a series of cables from his post in Moscow, including one of notable length. (Kennan had written his cables for the benefit of Secretary of Defense James V. Forrestal, a staunch early opponent of the Soviet Union.) After a long analysis of Soviet national character and diplomatic style, an analysis that remained the basis of American understandings for a generation, Kennan elaborated the principles of the strategy he thought appropriate in the novel (for Americans) circumstance of facing a powerful, uncommunicative, and unpredictable enemy in peacetime. In containment Kennan advised a stance toward the Soviet Union much like that which a father would urge on his son who daily had to face the malevolence of a low-class bully down the street. Be patient, the advice ran, and sooner or later peer pressure and maturity and self-confidence will result in more moderate and acceptable behavior. The bully will learn manners, discard the coarse and brutal in favor of the cultivated and refined.

But in the meantime be prepared to defend yourself. When the bully pushes you, push back, and if he strikes, respond equivalently, so that he will learn to respect you, perceive your strength, and aspire at first to behave more like you, then perhaps in some far off time, even to become your friend. The United States could expect the Soviet Union to behave with revolutionary instability and disregard for the niceties of international concourse, to seek its national security with fervor, and to probe continually for weaknesses in the Western countries grouped around the United States, in whom Russia's delusion found its grand focus. The United States would have to stand ready to meet those Soviet probes as and when they appeared, locally, and with commensurate force. At times stern speeches or even more subtle demonstrations of solidarity might suffice. But by 1947 it was almost certain that there would also be times when Americans, with their allies if possible, alone if necessary, would have to fight and die in combat with the advance guard of Soviet and international communism.

Within months the military aspects of the new containment policy were ubiquitous, at least as important as the diplomatic elements and in some cases more important. On the basis of the containment formula the United States responded to Soviet probes (as American policy makers of the era saw it) with the first military alliance system to which the nation had ever been a party in peacetime (with exception of the Franco-American alliance of 1778, which remained in effect until 1800, but which the United States refused to honor once its independence had been won). Concurrently, Americans resolved the first of many Berlin crises not by talking Soviet diplomats out of their intransigence, but by demonstrating that Russia and its client states could deny access to West Berlin only at the cost of large-scale military engagement, and that Western air power was more than adequate to supply the beleaguered citizens of West Berlin.

By January of 1950, a mere two and a half years after containment became the diplomatic policy of the United States, a military analog had been created, again with the help, even at the insistence, of the diplomatic establishment. In a recently declassified document of the National Security Council, the famous NSC-68 memorandum, American makers of policy determined to rebuild conventional military strength so that it would be possible to meet communist aggression in appropriate terms wherever in the world that might prove necessary. Barely six months after adoption of containment as policy, both the Policy Planning Staff of the State Department and the infant National Security Council, fearful that simple dependence on atomic monopoly might prove simple-minded, had inaugurated the study and discussion that resulted in NSC-68 proposals for a buildup of manpower and weaponry that was by American standards very large for peacetime.[7]

Kennan's containment and NSC-68 together comprised the elements of a national strategy for cold war in which the close link between diplomatic and military problems received confirmation. That link between diplomatic and military policies became the mark of successive attempts to compose national strategies that would preserve the security of the Western allies and limit the extent to which the Soviet Union and international communism could aggrandize themselves. And for a few years, at least through the Korean conflict in which the strategy was first tested, American policy seemed to have succeeded.

Subsequent developments called into question the extent of success in devising policy but not the tie between military and diplomatic policies. The end of nuclear monopoly, the more astounding end of thermonuclear monopoly, and the ensuing balance of terror in the middle fifties offered the frightening suggestion that Americans had done too little, too late. They faced a dimming future as, paralyzed by the balance of terror, they watched communism run rampant, triumphant over the small and weak nations that had trusted in the United States or had hoped, in some peaceable "third way," to keep themselves safe from communist aggression. As everyone knew, or as statesmen like Dean Acheson tried to explain, even the smaller nations of the world, especially of the industrialized world, could have great influence in the course of relations between the authoritarian communist East and the free democratic West. The sinews of national power were many—moral, military, economic. Acheson cautioned that if current trends in Soviet economic growth and bloc building both overt and covert continued, the time would come when the Soviet Union and its satellites would produce more steel than the West, with the consequence that communist plans for world domination would take on imminent reality.[8]

At center, of course, Americans were wrestling with an age-old complex question, that of the relation between force and diplomacy. Each new challenge they perceived to national security or to preeminence in world affairs caused them to reevaluate current strategy, to scrutinize that critical relation between the worlds of diplomacy and military operations, between peace and persuasion and war and coercion. The questions of scale introduced by development and deployment of nuclear weaponry further complicated the issue and obscured the classic nature of the deliberation. Discussions leading to the NSC-proposals of 1950 had begun with State Department planners declaring that, like their predecessors in the classic traditions of Western international relations, they needed military power, men in uniform trained and ready to support their diplomatic policies.

In the age of intercontinental ballistic missiles, of swollen Pentagon budgets, of intervention in Vietnam and elsewhere, it has been easy to suspect or at least to wonder whether that relation between force and diplomacy has reversed itself, with diplomacy sometimes an augmentation of and sometimes only a sideshow to the military power underlying national security and central to American foreign affairs. Under the conditions of cold war, because of the integration of military and diplomatic strategies and because of some of the assumptions that have marked diplomatic approaches to adversaries, especially communists, it is not unfair to conclude that theorists and practitioners of force, the military services and their representatives, have come to outweigh diplomats in American policy.

4| New Foreign Affairs Agencies

Over time, Secretary Hull's distinction between policy and operations, the wartime integration of diplomacy and strategy, and the conditions of cold war foreign relations contributed to the inception and growth of new agencies in American foreign affairs, powerful agencies independent of the State Department. The idea had been attractive that the work of the diplomat was mental, that diplomacy depended on brain power, quick thinking, the kind of political insight that came only from men of the right type who had experience in foreign relations. In practice the people who had emphasized day-to-day decisions and actions proved more adept than the members of Hull's department. They did not merely take over operations. Each of the many agencies and officers that became involved in operations influenced policy and in some instances originated policy.

In the handling of American foreign relations two kinds of new agencies developed in addition to expansion of foreign interests in several traditional government departments such as Treasury, Agriculture, and Commerce. During the war and immediately afterward, agencies with a clearly operational character grew up to carry on the enormous business of an alliance at war and then the business of trying to make peace and reconstituting shattered economies and governments. Later, another group of new agencies developed with purposes more competitive with the functions and responsibilities that Hull and his department had mistakenly expected to monopolize. The Agency for International Development and the United States Information Agency were in the first category; the National Security Council with all its subsidiary and associated committees and staffs was the principal organization of the second type. Crossing the division between operations and policy, the Central Intelligence Agency and the other intelligence-action agencies, military and civilian, possessed unclear responsibilities.

The proliferating defense, intelligence, foreign aid, information, and national security agencies tend to confuse the inquiring student. In fact, they confused the State Department. Had the agencies robbed the department of its power? Or had the agencies acquired influence because of inadequency in State? In one area, foreign operations, the answer seemed clear. The State Department had lost control of foreign operations, had given way not only to the military but to a host of other agencies, some new, some old, and all troublesome, busy, and (the unkindest cut of all) better funded than State.

Many a novel has been written, many a diplomat has complained, about the inability of the State Department to control these other representatives of the United States and to ensure that there would ensue no untoward incidents. One can smile knowingly at mention of the CIA and its adventures, but it is far from the only agency to produce problems. Even the Peace Corps, well-meant and for the most part well-received, could create unpleasantness. As one diplomat remarked, it achieved a place in the American mind "somewhere between the Boy Scouts and motherhood." There nonetheless were several contretemps arising out of its activity. It will be a long time before some people in State, and some in the various host countries, forget the approach of early corpsmen, an attitude summed up by Ellis Briggs as a determination to go out and "wreak good on some native," a globe-girdling expansion of the *boyscoutismo,* which had passed for policy toward the Latin American countries.[9]

There is the notable story of Peace Corps volunteers to Turkey, who upon receiving as a gift a portrait of Kemal Atatürk, the father of modern Turkey, placed it over their commode. When the local mayor, proud of the preparation his village had made for the volunteers, came to inspect the plumbing—the only such arrangement in the village—his outrage was so great that the volunteers had to quit Turkey.

Embarrassment worries State Department officers much less than lack of knowledge, confusion, cross-purposes, redundancy, or omissions when too many agencies carry on foreign relations. It is sobering to learn that there are six separate staffs in the Pentagon, all concerned with foreign affairs, which together possess both manpower and budget larger than the State Department. One department desk officer, concerned with relations with just one small African country, calculated in the late 1960s that there were at least sixteen other people in Washington doing almost exactly the same thing, each in his cubbyhole in his separate agency doing his redundant work, never communicating with his fellow African-country-watchers.

Every President since World War II, as well as every secretary of state, has considered an ineffectual, sprawling State Department intolerable but probably beyond correction. Most Presidents and secretaries enter office with the best intentions of straightening things out, for they realize more than many members of the Foreign Service will admit that a strong department and service could be invaluable. But the confusion of the overlapping bureaucracies, the sheer enormity of the reformer's task, and the inertia of organizations set in their ways, all mean that the reform and strengthening of State and the reordering of processes will be slow and require far more time than most chief executives can ever afford. When a new President discovers, if he did not suspect it, that the making of foreign policy resembles a taffy pull, that the department reminds some senior officials of "an unusually well-staffed hospital," he is likely to respond in predictable ways.[10] First, in his ritual address to the Foreign Service he will hold out the prospect of a reformed, strong service and department as his right hand in foreign policy and foreign relations. Then, when the men he appoints to bring this vision down to earth fail or take too long or when some urgent problem arises, presidential patience and good intentions will diminish at equal rates, to be replaced by presidential improvisation in a determined effort to solve problems before it is too late, to make policy somehow, even if not through the Department of State.

But some conditions in the State Department became too bad not to correct, no matter how difficult or drastic the remedy. Once in 1961 someone at the White House had asked the State Department for a statement of policy on British Guiana, where a change of government seemed about to occur. The President was told that the statement could not possibly be ready in less than a week or two.

> It would have to be drafted, and then it would have to move up through the various levels of Inter-American Affairs. Then there would be clearances and concurrences—European Affairs, International Organization Affairs, Intelligence and Research, Political Affairs. Then when it got up near the Secretary's level, there would be interagency clearances—the Pentagon, the Central Intelligence Agency, maybe Treasury or Commerce. And finally the paper would have to be cleared by the National Security Council.[11]

In the postwar era perhaps the only factor that saved the State Department from powerlessness and obscurity was the fact, already mentioned, that several Presidents appointed strong secretaries of state. No one could altogether ignore their departments, which in a sense meant their personal prerogatives, so long as they occupied the office of the secretary. They could just pick up the red phone and call the Oval Office. Unfortunately, the influential secretaries often were not particularly good administrators. Especially under Dulles the department and the Foreign Service deteriorated in morale and perhaps in quality and fell into organizational disarray as a result of postwar additions of personnel. Dulles frequently displayed contempt for his own department, allowed men like Kennan to leave the Foreign Service, and generally dealt with subordinates in a superior manner.

When Nixon took office it seemed clear that quick reaction—or any policy other than that of consensus, the policy of the lowest common denominator—could not come out of the traditional establishment. He and Kissinger decided to make the National Security Council, a smaller, perhaps more versatile organization, the center of their discussions and decisions. They hoped to avoid the delay, indecision, and consensus politics of the traditional bureaucracy. They also hoped to find a way to make decisions effective, to ensure that what had been decided was done and not just absorbed, swallowed, or lost. The NSC had been created in 1947 as a high-level body in which it would be possible to seek the kind of diplomatic and military strategies that the cold war seemed to call for. In that council the President or his delegate, the Vice President, the secretaries of state and defense (newly organized as a combination of the three services in 1947), and the director of the little-known Office of Emergency Preparedness were to consider the questions of national policy that transcended the interests or competence of individual agencies. The NSC in 1947 was readily recognizable as an imitation of the Joint State-War-Navy Coordinating Committee in which so many of the critical issues of wartime had been debated.* Like that earlier committee it had an uneven use and influence. Truman employed the NSC to study several important questions but came to rely on the succession of strong individuals he named to head the State Department. Eisenhower rejuvenated the NSC, convened it almost weekly, and seems to have taken a leading part in its work despite the power and prominence of Secretary Dulles. Under Kennedy and Johnson the NSC was summoned into session infrequently, on occasion with urgency. It did not expand into a full system with subordinate agencies and bureaucracies of its own until the Nixon era.

Ironically, the proliferation of agencies under Nixon's reinvigorated NSC raised the possibility that what had begun as an attempt to circumvent bureaucracies might turn into another bureaucracy. The NSC staff grew to more than a hundred people, with a half-dozen committees or agencies, a system complicated enough so that President Nixon felt obliged to explain it in detail in each of his annual messages to Congress on foreign affairs.

The Nixon-Kissinger NSC system did not, as some critics have asserted, supplant the older agencies, particularly the State Department, nor did it suppress the alternative suggestions and interests of agencies other than State and Defense. If it worked it was supposed to provide opportunity for interested agencies to have a voice in discussions; more important, it was supposed to ensure

---

* The statute creating the NSC originally named the Director of Defense Mobilization as a member. It also placed the CIA and the Joint Chiefs of Staff into official support of the NSC's work.

that alternatives reached the top of the system instead of being suppressed or merged in the bureaucratic search for consensus that the practice of clearances and concurrences had represented.

As Nixon explained to Congress, the NSC system began to work when he, or his national security adviser, or the NSC itself, assigned a problem or topic to an Interdepartmental Group. Such a group would have members from all agencies that had, or thought they should have, something to say about the issue, and in acknowledgment of State's preeminence in foreign affairs such groups were chaired by an assistant secretary of state, whichever assistant secretary was most appropriate for the subject. The Interdepartmental Group was to carry on "intensive study, . . . formulate policy choices and to analyze the pros and cons of different courses of action." The report of the Interdepartmental Group went to a second interagency unit, the Senior Review Group chaired by Kissinger, "to insure that the issues, options, and views are presented fully and fairly." Finally, the results of the first two groups' deliberations were presented to the President and the NSC.[12]

There were several variations in the NSC's operations. Some issues were too special for Interdepartmental Groups and came to the National Security Council via a different route. Matters of defense, especially technical questions, were reviewed in the NSC Defense Program Review Committee at the undersecretary level. A Verification Panel gathered information and established facts pertaining to strategic arms limitation, an important task in the years when preparation for the negotiation of SALT I was going forward. Similarly, during the last years of involvement in Vietnam, the Vietnam Special Studies Group gathered and presented "to the highest levels of the United States government the fullest and most up-to-date information on trends and conditions in the countryside in Vietnam." [13] One of the most important organizations subordinate to the National Security Council, the Washington Special Actions Group, received responsibility for "crisis management." Composed of senior officers from government agencies, WSAG drafted contingency plans, attempted to foresee crises or urgent situations within a two- to four-year period, and formed a nucleus around which task forces for management of crises would be constructed.

After only a year of operating his new NSC system, Nixon found it necessary to tinker again with the mechanism. He created the Under Secretaries Committee, which received the unenviable assignment of "linking the process of policy formulation to the operations of government." [14] In typical bureaucratic language Nixon said that not enough of what he and the NSC decided was affecting the agencies operating abroad or participating in American policy. So undersecretaries—the number-two men—in cabinet and non-cabinet agencies were ordered to insure that decisions and actions taken in their own agencies were consistent with policies that had been defined in the NSC. Perhaps even more difficult, the undersecretaries were supposed to devise operational alternatives to those proposed or ordered by the NSC or to develop in detail the execution of decision within the guidelines outlined by the NSC. And there have been other emendations to the NSC's organization. In the third year of the new system Nixon created an Intelligence Committee to advise on the "quality, scope, and timeliness of the intelligence input into presidential decisions, and on the steps to improve it." [15] With that organization the NSC system stood complete. In the summer of 1974, the President resigned. Presumably Gerald Ford and other successors would try other ideas if Nixonian notions did not suffice.

And so the making of policy, as well as the carrying out of policy, has moved constantly away from the Department of State during the thirty years that have passed since the end of World War II. The reasons for this departure of both policy and operations are many and varied, and there is no point in repeating them. What they have added up to, however, is a large change in the practice of the federal government. No longer can the secretary of state speak as the first officer of the President's cabinet, secure in knowledge that whatever he says will go straight to the President and very probably become policy. Instead, it will go to the National Security Council and there, perhaps, get lost.

CHAPTER FOUR | Conducting Foreign Relations

Although the results rather than the ways of diplomacy have properly claimed the attention of historians, the formal organization of the diplomatic mission and the day-to-day work, unofficial and official, of individual diplomats deserve analysis in their own right. To establish and maintain diplomatic relations is neither easy nor cheap. Governments must expend much effort and money to conduct foreign affairs conveniently and satisfactorily. But there is, of course, far more to diplomacy than organization. For individuals to perform all the tasks and meet all the responsibilities that fall to the ordinary diplomat is immensely difficult. A member of the American Foreign Service must arrange for his family to move into a strange and often inconvenient environment—where housing is not always easy or problems of health may arise. Then he and his family will encounter the demands of social life in a foreign capital, demands that can occupy a great deal of time and energy. When he turns to his work in the office, he will encounter huge masses of paper, which somehow or other must be moved from place to place. Once the embassy has been organized and the funds duly expended to set the wheels in motion, the representative of the Foreign Service—on hand with family, suitably or unsuitably domiciled, healthy or not, the paperwork in order—must then turn to the business of observing, reporting, and negotiating.

1| Constituting a Mission

After resolution of the problems involved in decisions on recognition of governments but before the work of diplomatic relations can begin, the governments concerned must establish missions. In recent times this task has become complex, for the varied and extensive work of diplomacy seems to require an immense amount of organization.

The principal mission sent to the capital of a foreign country to carry on business with the central government is called an embassy. The distinction between an embassy and a legation was formerly of some importance. An embassy is headed by an ambassador whereas a legation is directed by a minister, a lower-ranking diplomat. Formerly countries would send embassies only to those states with whom they had important relations; legations were sent to countries of lesser importance. But in the years between the world wars many of the smaller states began to long for the signs of status and importance, the panoply of formal relations at the highest level. In recognition of that sort of national pride, and as an elaborate (and one must add expensive) compliment, the United States and many other nations replaced almost all legations with embassies. One should perhaps add that in terms of personnel this change was sometimes awkward. Suddenly there was need in American diplomacy for more ambassadors than ever before, and a great many men who had risen to the rank of minister were quickly elevated one more notch, to the exalted rank of ambassador. Some of them kept their sense of proportion sufficiently to realize that calling a mission an embassy rather than a legation might soothe the host government but not really change the importance of relations with it (or, consequently, the real importance of the head of mission). Others of the new ambassadors found their new title vastly satisfying and tended to make fools of themselves. "Sumner's shambassadors," such newly elevated men were called, after Sumner Welles, the undersecretary of state in the late 1930s who had urged the raising of American legations in Latin American countries to embassies.

Embassies may be large or small; but the only real difference in organization of the post is that there is more of it in a large one. There are the same titles and offices from post to post. An embassy is headed by an ambassador, either a political appointee, a Foreign Service officer with the rank of career ambassador, or in the case of countries of secondary importance, a Foreign Service officer ranking somewhere between career minister and FSO-3 and carrying ambassadorial rank only for the duration of his assignment. In embassies of moderate to large size, the ambassador is advised by a counselor, an experienced Foreign Service officer of high rank, usually a career minister or a Foreign Service officer class one at the largest posts. (The Foreign Service ranks begin with 8 and ascend to FSO-1.) Then there are, as in traditional times, secretaries of embassy—first secretary, second secretary, and in large missions even third secretary, each with assigned areas of responsibility. In British and American practice third secretaryships used to be reserved for well-connected younger sons and dilettantes who intended to spend only a couple of years abroad before going into business. Some observers now say that the first secretary of an American embassy is likely to be the station chief of the CIA. In large missions there are also numerous Foreign Service officers at work on political, economic, and administrative matters, gathering information, pushing paper, taking part in the social whirl, chairing meetings. The mission also will boast several attachés attached to the mission but working for another government department, such as military attachés or men from departments such as Labor, Agriculture, and Commerce. (Foreign Service officers sometimes function as labor and commerce attachés.) The attachés busily gather information. And in addition there may be hangers-on from the Agency for International Development, the State Department's own Arms Control and Disarmament Agency, or representatives related to United States-United Nations activities, such as the Food and Agricultural Organization. The possibilities are nearly limitless, which is why, with clerical staff, some American missions contain almost a thousand people.

In nearly every embassy today there is a specially designated officer whose work differs greatly from that of almost everyone else—the cultural attaché, usually from the United States Information Agency. In smaller posts he may be called a PAO (public affairs officer). While other diplomats collect information, the cultural officer gives it out. With the help of the local United States Information Service staff, a cultural attaché or public affairs officer answers the many requests for information and materials about the United States, travels and lectures, perhaps writes an occasional essay or article for the popular press in the host country. At the same time the attaché may interpret the culture and attitudes of the host nation to his associates, for ideally the department appoints men or women unusually well-acquainted with countries in which they serve. Of course the entire staff of a diplomatic mission represents American personality and culture. They will, justly or not, be taken as typical or even stereotypical, and beyond doubt their behavior and attitudes make greater and more lasting impressions than the writings and lectures of a single attaché. But it does help to have an expert, specially designated, to observe internal confusions and to define and carry out the cultural purposes of his assigned embassy.

In addition to embassies there are consulates, offices usually of smaller dimension and simpler organization sent to deal with local, not central, authorities in foreign countries and concerned mostly with questions of business, commerce, law, and the protection of American citizens in the regions and large cities of a country. In more important cities, sometimes to supervise a number of consulates, the United States maintains a consulate general, which is really just a large consulate. A consul general will have several consular officers as assistants, and each consulate throughout the country will have one or more consular officers and perhaps a modest staff of clerks, typists, and translators.

All of these missions—embassies, consulates general, consulates —are expensive to maintain. Measured in terms of Washington appropriations and compared with the budgets of some other cabinet departments and sub-cabinet agencies, the Department of State does not spend much money. But in any other terms, in any other city, the sums of money would seem considerable. The stark figures are large enough to impress one with the responsibility that falls to American diplomats who must expend them, and so it is interesting to see just what it costs to carry on diplomatic relations. Costs vary greatly from country to country, roughly corresponding to the extent of American diplomatic business and thus of personnel. For example, in 1972 in Iceland, a small but strategic country, the department spent $447,873, of which about 40 percent was for the salaries of the fifteen diplomats posted there. In Iceland the United States Information Agency with its cultural and informational programs spent another $144,837, for a grand total of $592,710. Somewhat less than one percent of that sum, $5,100, was for representation costs, entertainments that officials of the United States must proffer to Icelanders, fellow diplomats, visiting Americans, and junketing congressmen.[1]

The modesty of expenditure in Iceland, or in small countries in less developed areas of the world, hardly compares with monies required to carry on diplomatic affairs in larger and more important states, especially those in which the government maintains many consulates or those handful of capitals in which the world's most pressing business is transacted. In Canada, a nearby friendly nation in which the United States in the year 1972 had ninety-seven representatives of the Department of State and the United States Information Service, the cost of programs and administrative expenses, salaries, and representation allowances ($15,700) came to slightly under $4 million. Since World War II the communist countries have tended to discourage large diplomatic missions from Western powers, which may be one reason that costs for diplomatic missions there are lower than for Western states equivalent in size and importance. In Poland, the expenses for 1972 were slightly under $2 million (not including the salary of a solitary American Seabee, whose stationing there may seem a cause for wonder; actually, he checks for electronic "bugs" in the embassy).

From the modest budgets and staffs for countries such as Iceland, Canada, and Poland, there is a great leap forward to those for centers of diplomatic life, such as Italy, or for that no-man's-land of the cold war, West Germany. Consulates general in Milan and Naples yearly spend more than the annual appropriation for Iceland, and the consulate general in Palermo nearly as much. The total for American diplomatic operations in Italy (excluding operations of cabinet departments other than State) was $10 million. In West Germany, where there were more than two hundred American diplomatic representatives and staff, appropriations were half again as much, slightly more than $14 million, even before inclusion of the $3.5 million USIA budget. In countries like West Germany and Italy an ambassador receives a representation allowance of more than $35,000, and even though it is seven times the allowance for Iceland it is less than half of the allowance a British diplomat there ordinarily would receive.

Are the costs of diplomatic representation too high? That question causes trouble between department representatives and the members of Congress each year when it is time for reconsideration of the budget. Perhaps no good answer is possible. All too often diplomacy has no tangible product, at least not the kind that one can see as a commodity with a price or as a correlation between monies allocated and spent and results obtained. A so-called technical sensor, a spy satellite of the sort lofted every few weeks by the United States and the Soviet Union, can take hundreds or even thousands of pictures per hour and wondrously transmit them to earth for evaluation by both machines and humans. A diplomat may produce no pictures at all (a great liability when dealing with the Congress) and only an occasional tidbit of information that is complete enough in itself to be sensational or even noteworthy. But a spy satellite cannot handle the many, many tasks that a modern-day diplomat must deal with. And it is to the hectic life and the extraordinary tasks of a diplomat that we now must turn.

2| Going Abroad

Diplomacy begins with the simplest fact of foreign relations: life abroad, the very special life of a diplomat. The custom of maintaining diplomatic representatives in foreign countries is of recent origin in comparison with the long history of relations among sovereign states. In the early days of diplomacy, to be a diplomat was a fairly simple proposition. In an era when diplomatic missions were specific and of short duration, an emissary could readily make his abode in rented or borrowed quarters—suitable to his station and his sovereign's dignity, to be sure. Occasionally he might even become the guest of the sovereign to whom he had been sent. And he left his family at home. For centuries it was a rule of Venetian diplomacy that an ambassador had to leave his wife and family while he conducted business abroad. Venetians believed that wives and families were perhaps too expensive and distracting, too demanding of a man's time while he performed public service. How domestic freedom must have liberated the Venetian diplomat to play the games of intrigue and enticement so much a part of the diplomacy of centuries past! It is no mere speculation also to say that many diplomats today might be better off were such a regulation in force, because they could avoid the demands of socially inclined females who cannot adjust to inhospitable climates, provincial locations, or other privations, who measure their husbands' success by the nondiplomatic attractions of their posts.

As permanent representation became customary, diplomats necessarily or at least usually began to take their families along. Then the problems appeared. Consider the business of transportation in the years before the twentieth century. Vast portions of the world—the Near East, the Far East, and Africa—had no roads, much less motorcars, and some capitals were virtually inaccessible. As late as the end of the last century, an American assigned as minister to Persia could find no company to arrange his passage. He finally acquired directions, though not arrangements, from his predecessor at the post. All semblance of modernity ended at the Bosporus, and thereafter for hundreds of trackless miles across mountain and desert he and his bride, their 145 pieces of luggage, and their grand piano proceeded by camel packtrain to greet the King of Kings in Teheran.

Today's diplomatic family can now easily solve most problems of transportation, but there are other difficulties in taking a family abroad and making life bearable, especially for the young Foreign Service officer, whose income is modest. Many an officer arrives at his new post flat broke from outfitting his family with the unusual clothing, utensils, and other supplies they will need or which they think they will need. Once at his assigned location the new officer must not only report in but he must find housing and perhaps household staff in an area where the diplomatic community has already strained or even exhausted the market in both. Villas on the Mediterranean, charming from a distance, all too often prove dark and mildewed inside, like too many parts of a diplomat's world, "long on picturesqueness and short on plumbing," too far from town and office and exorbitant in rent.[2]

Nor are chiefs of mission spared the domestic problems faced by junior officers. Perhaps the first thing an ambassador must do at his new post is inspect, repair, and redecorate. William E. Dodd, ambassador to Germany in 1933–1937, spent considerable time arranging for a new building as his official residence, the Bluecher Palace. Construction of partitions, pay rates for local laborers and craftsmen, even paint colors became the subjects of cable interchange between Dodd and the department in Washington. The problems took years to solve.

The most trivial difficulties of household arrangements have plagued ambassadors, sometimes at moments when their attention should have been elsewhere. One of the first cables from Dodd's successor in Berlin, Hugh R. Wilson, concerned an inventory of the embassy's glassware accompanied by a query as to whether the discrepancies should not be charged to Dodd. Wilson in 1938 was not enough alarmed by the war scare of September—the Munich crisis—to interrupt his attempts to have his bedroom furniture shipped from New York.

The next step after making a residence habitable—for an ambassador or his assistants—is staffing it. It is difficult for Americans who have not lived abroad to understand why the subject of servants, their availability and relative merits, likes and dislikes, the way in which one has to deal with them, should figure so prominently in discussions of the life diplomatic. The topic looms large in many memoirs, and a Foreign Service wife rarely fails to inquire about or remark such things at each stop in the diplomatic shuffle. It comes as a shock to learn that it took fourteen servants to run the six-room American ambassadorial residence in New Delhi, and proportionately high ratios of servants exist at many other such posts. All members of an ambassador's staff have similar problems, if lesser in scale. Only with experience, or with reflection, does one begin to consider the labor, the time-consuming and arduous tasks of the household in countries where there is no running water, or where heat for water and for the domicile comes from chopped wood, where there is little or no refrigeration and food must be bought daily in crowded markets and scattered shops. There are few capitals in which the American homemaker, accustomed to all manner of labor-saving and time-saving devices, would find it easy to take proper care of her family, much less play any helping role in her husband's professional life.

Ironically, the problems of servants are often considerably lessened in countries where the political work of diplomacy is difficult, the communist countries of the world. In some of those countries, which are virtual police states, servants for foreign diplomatic missions are often under orders from their own governments to spy on or otherwise observe the doings of their employers. In effect they are captives in their jobs, and as one American diplomat gleefully noted, they cannot quit, no matter how hard one works them. Whether terrified of their own state security services or dedicated to them, such servants are at least dependable.

The health of diplomatic personnel also presents problems in overseas posts. Children have to be born. People threaten to, and sometimes do, die. Or perhaps teeth have to be filled. The ambassador to Russia in the early 1930s, William C. Bullitt, once described his worries about his assistants' teeth. The only three tolerably good dentists in Moscow at that time, to whom the diplomatic community naturally went, had suffered exile, leaving some members of the embassy "hanging on to temporary fillings." [3] Foreign Service families come almost to expect that over the years they will have to sacrifice some of their health as a result of the life they lead. The most common illness, amoebic dysentery, or Delhi belly (there is a special name for it in all the Eastern countries: gyppy tummy, the turkey trots, the Khartoums), strikes nearly everyone sooner or later, sometimes to become chronic and ultimately debilitating.

Another concern for diplomats overseas is obtaining sufficient supplies of the local currency. In foreign countries, diplomatic personnel and missions contract for goods and services in local money, and salaries and budgets are pegged to cost-of-living scales. When the cost of living or the value of currency changes, a diplomat is in trouble. Sometimes he must sell dollars on the black market, a violation of Foreign Service rules. In many countries the diplomatic officer may suffer real disadvantage if he is required to turn in his salary check for local currency at the official rate of exchange, often much less favorable than black market exchange rates. The only recourse, short of unconscionable costs, is the black market.

The diplomat who has survived transposition into a foreign environment, found housing, staffed it, and made tolerable health arrangements will have still other concerns. One of the most important, both for himself and his family, will be that he may discover that he has almost no privacy. Depending on the locality, diplomats may be made to feel like goldfish, having no private lives of their own, their every word and action a source of wonderment to some chance spectator. Americans, who come from a huge country where there is, by world standards, a great deal of privacy, can easily undergo traumatic experience in the closely crowded capitals of foreign nations. In this regard modern embassy architecture is no help. The bright steel and glass buildings constructed for American embassies and residences in recent years were not designed to enhance privacy. Henry Villard has told of prolonged and vain efforts to obtain curtains to cover some of the many windows in the new embassy in Dakar. All appeals were without effect until he cabled the department that from the one seat in his bathroom he had a magnificent view of the city, and the city had a magnificent view of him.

The transition abroad can have a shattering effect upon the ordinary American's sense of privacy. In some localities every stranger meets suspicion, perhaps outright hostility, which may pose a greater personal hazard than the polite prying of the central government. Only beginner's Arabic saved Foreign Service officer Earle Russell, Jr., from spending time in a backcountry Lebanese jail when local police noticed that he was not only a stranger, traveling by donkey in the hinterlands, but that he possessed a camera. His story—that he was an American diplomat taking a vacation—hardly seemed credible and was surely poor cover for the spy the Lebanese believed him to be.

All of the foregoing problems would be enough to deter most individuals from a diplomatic career, that is, if they knew much about them in advance. In fact, it takes a special sort of family to savor a life that is so filled with practical obstructions. The diplomat, therefore, needs a cooperative family. It takes a family that can travel with calm, and, perhaps after enough experience, with aplomb, a family that can adapt to new quarters, new cultures, and problems seemingly without end and certainly beyond expectation. But the result can be—and this is the purpose of diplomatic representation—new friends, a better international environment in which Americans as a nation face the vastly diverse peoples of the world.

3| Social Life

The one aspect of diplomatic work that is least understood from the outside is social life. There is considerable debate on just how important or useful entertainment may be in diplomacy. But there is no argument over whether diplomats have a great deal of social life.

A few diplomats—and many congressmen and private citizens —have become convinced that diplomatic entertainment is an expensive waste of time (though congressmen on junkets and Americans abroad always expect the ambassador to produce his private bottle of Scotch when they drop in). Hence the descriptions commonly applied to diplomats by Americans who call them cookie-pushers and "white-spats boys," the description used by President Harry S Truman. But most diplomats believe that the descriptions of striped-pants incompetents obscure the importance of entertainment in their work. Chester Bowles, a former ambassador to India, used entertainment to "keep in touch with foreign diplomats, members of Parliament, ministers and civil servants, businessmen, educators, and welfare workers whom we might otherwise not see." [4] The Bowles' successors, the Galbraiths, found they were either entertaining or being entertained nearly every day at both luncheon and dinner, the latter, by the way, quite late and after a cocktail hour that constituted still another obligatory appearance.

Most important, and perhaps most numerous of the *de rigueur* social occasions, are the national-day celebrations of the many countries of the world. Just as the United States celebrates July 4 as a great patriotic festival, nearly every nation has a date similarly hallowed. And as United States envoys celebrate July 4 with local Americans and with the diplomatic corps, each nation large and small observes its day with ceremony, not complete without the respectful attention and attendance of representatives of nations with which such a country may have diplomatic relations. No diplomatic occasion is more important, more requisite of ambassadorial presence. For a country such as the United States, in diplomatic relations with most of the countries of the world, the number of such occasions in a major capital places an extraordinary demand on the time of mission personnel, though perhaps it does not pose as great a problem as for the leaders of each new revolution, coup, or successor government who must select a national day to celebrate that is not already spoken for on the international calendar. And there are other less predictable but sometimes even more important ceremonial occasions that require at least a high-level representative from a diplomatic mission and may demand even more in the way of time and solicitude. When sovereigns are crowned or (more the case nowadays) when heads of state celebrate birthdays or other personal anniversaries, officials of friendly states must dance attendance.

Some occasions call for elaborate gifts, and here there can be large problems. Most people have one or two friends for whom it is difficult to shop, people who seem to have everything. Imagine the difficulty of devising a suitable present for a diplomatic personage. Gift-giving between heads of state, of course, has become a ridiculous competition for originality and ostentation. Nikita Khrushchev perhaps won the contest for originality when he presented the Kennedy family with a puppy born of Strelka, the dog the Russians had orbited in space on August 19, 1960. An award for the least appropriate gift may belong to President Eisenhower and his secretary of state, John Foster Dulles, for their presentation of a .32 caliber automatic pistol to General Mohammed Naguib of Egypt, inscribed "from his friend Dwight D. Eisenhower." The gift was made at a troubled time in the Middle East, which prompted Dulles to remark as he gave Naguib the pistol: "This is for keeping the peace, not for war." Naguib drily replied, "I know." [5] There was ostentation on both sides in the famous exchange of animals between President Nixon and Chinese Premier Chou En-lai, a pair of musk oxen for the Chinese and a pair of giant pandas for the Americans. As *The New York Times* wrote of the exchange: "Mr. Nixon has shown the greatest degree of imagination in this area since the King of Siam sent Abraham Lincoln a white elephant. One can only hope that a century from now 'musk oxen' will not be Chinese for a useless object that can't be disposed of." [6]

One might remark parenthetically that in diplomacy the entertainments, like the gifts, can verge on the bizarre, perhaps because diplomats in the sheer perplexity of what to do next in order to catch attention sometimes have gone beyond the borders of good taste. Ambassador William C. Bullitt in Moscow during the early 1930s bragged of the entertainment he provided, and surely it was of a sort that the penurious Congress of the Great Depression never would have underwritten; only a millionaire like Bullitt could have done such a thing:

> There was a good turnout for the ball I gave. . . . Litvinov came with his wife and eldest daughter. It was an astonishingly successful party, thoroughly dignified yet gay. Everyone happy and no one drunk. . . . We got a thousand tulips from Helsingfors and forced a lot of birch trees into premature leafage and arranged one end of the dining room as a collective farm with peasant accordion players, dancers, and all sorts of baby things, such as birds, goats, and a couple of infant bears about the size of cats. We also had pleasant lighting effects done by the best theater here and a bit of a cabaret. It was really great fun and the Turkish Ambassador and about twenty others remained until breakfast at eight.[7]

The occasions, bizarre and otherwise—the socializing—go on and on, and once in a while dangers arise. Liquor poses two hazards: It does things to people, and even worse, it causes people to do things. Too much drinking is hard on the body, as one French diplomat noted at the end of his time in Washington. "God help a diplomat's digestive tract," he said, "for in service to my country I have consumed 35,000 cocktails in the last decade." But the other hazard, the unpredictable actions of people under the influence, is far more a matter of concern. Probably no diplomats suffer more or have more to fear in this regard than Americans. Memoirs are replete with stories of visiting congressmen who became difficult when under the influence, and some have become notorious for drunken, insulting conduct. Senator Key Pittman, sometime chairman of the Foreign Relations Committee, is perhaps best remembered for chasing a State Department official down the corridors of Claridge's during the London Economic Conference of 1933. Some years later a drunken congressman at a formal state entertainment in Greece patted Queen Frederika affectionately and pronounced her the cutest little Queenie he had ever seen.[8]

The social life of a proper diplomat is a demanding part of his work. It is hard to make time in the calendar of obligatory social functions to see friends. Like other people leading less complicated social lives, diplomats have friends, people with whom they like to spend an evening and with whom they can let down their guard for a few hours, speaking freely and being themselves. But especially for junior officers there are the almost constant demands upon time, and many of the demands are unanticipated. For no matter what plans one might have made, a junior officer cannot refuse a social invitation or assignment that comes from his superior. All Foreign Service wives can tell of parties abandoned, dinners called off, friends put off time and again because suddenly the ambassador needs an extra man or an extra couple at his table. Here the aspect of entertainment as duty begins to show.

4| Routine Diplomacy

Arduous transpositions and social whirls are only prefatory, or perhaps ancillary, to the voluminous and complex work of diplomacy. One comes then to what in American parlance is called "the job." And so much of the job, contrary to popular belief, is sheer routine.

Consider the problem of paperwork. The volume of paper since World War II has increased immensely. The paper flow became so oppressive after the war that the department in 1961 and in following years undertook to study the handling of internal and external mail. Some of the findings were startling. In 1961 one out of every thirteen department employees in Washington, a total of 464 people, was employed full time in sorting and distributing mail. Including all copies made, delivered, and filed in the department, the mail totaled 99.4 million pieces per year. A study committee of officials and outside experts finally altered the handling and distribution of paper by applying the efficiency expert's stopwatch and counting devices and redrawing the delivery routes of internal mailmen. An incidental result was the restructuring of regulations on distribution of classified documents. It was common not so many years ago to make as many as eighty copies of top-secret communications. The department now makes fewer copies, and very few copies indeed of documents with such esoteric classifications as "nodis" and "limdis." [9]

The business of communication, of which paperwork is a part, has forced the introduction of all sorts of mechanical devices to assist the flow of information. The necessity for high-speed and high-security communication has made the department the possessor of elaborate, costly, and continually updated communications facilities maintained in security within the main building in Washington. In the operations center on the seventh floor, departmental officers of the highest reliability keep watch twenty-four hours a day, reading the incoming top-secret material from diplomatic and intelligence sources around the world. Watch officers feed the information to State's Bureau of Intelligence and Research, where the information is evaluated and interpreted. The department maintains another complete communications room on the fifth floor, which handles the remaining communications traffic urgent enough to require the speed of cable transmission but not so highly classified as to pass through the more secure facilities of the operations center. There officers process the bulk of the more than 400,000 telegrams received and sent annually in the department. A great portion of the raw data coming into the fifth-floor room is of little interest to State. There is a practical division of the data among State, the DIA (Defense Intelligence Agency), and the CIA in which State concentrates on political intelligence, the DIA on military, and the CIA on technical and economic intelligence. The CIA relies heavily on the reports of diplomatic personnel.

Inevitably, it seems, new ways of doing things cost more than old ways, and so it is with modern communications. The price of a fast-paced world has risen steadily and has become almost a sort of "J" factor, which can upset even the best-laid financial plans of mission chiefs, bureaus, and the department itself. Although in the department it is frequently said that crisis is the normal state of affairs, the volume of work does fluctuate, which places irregular demands on the budget allotments of posts. It is not unusual for an ambassador to have to request an immediate augmentation of his cable fund. Protection of American citizens, sometimes of a single American, can generate several hundred documents, perhaps half of which come via expensive cable. A rise in telegraphic traffic can wreck a post's budget if it occurs late in a fiscal period. In a unique case early in the cold war, an American consul deep in the hinterland of the Near East became his government's only source of information about Soviet and communist military movements and intentions in the touchy diplomacy surrounding the Soviet penetration of Iran and American demands for a reversal of the incursion. Consul Robert Rossow in Azerbaijan incurred telegraph bills of between $10,000 and $15,000 a month while he reported on local but globally important conditions. In those unsettled times only cash payment of so large a bill was acceptable, and, as it turned out, the communist puppet government of the People's Republic of Azerbaijan could not pay its own employees until, each month, Rossow had paid his telegraph bill.

In addition to the constant business—and busyness—of communication between Washington and the missions abroad, which sometimes appears to occupy all the time of embassy personnel, there is always other paperwork, such as the interminable visas— the issuing of visas to individuals who for one reason or another, good or bad or indifferent, want to come to the United States. Issuance of a visa is not an automatic or simple affair. Visas can be issued only in accord with the immigration laws of the United States, which specify the reasons for which people may visit the United States and which limit the time they may spend for these purposes. Travelers, students, people visiting relatives, businessmen, all must comply with detailed regulations. Foreign students in the United States may not hold jobs, so that they do not offer their labor or services in competition with Americans who might be seeking employment, nor may they remain in the country for more than two years. People who enter the United States under a temporary visa are monitored so that, whether through carelessness or design, they do not extend their stay or become permanent residents of the United States without conforming to immigration laws, which contain another group of restrictions on access to this country.

Visa work involves much more than issuing visas to applicants. Diplomatic officers stationed in foreign countries possess the major responsibility for ascertaining that an applicant makes no false pretense either in intentions or in identity, whether for violation of immigration restrictions or even perhaps for insinuation into the United States as a foreign agent. In this latter sense consular officials are a first line of defense against intruders. Customarily the consular officer will interrogate a visa applicant as to his family circumstances, profession, interest, and intent in visiting the United States, and then for verification of identity elicit a short biography including especially a history of employment and domicile. Although a consular officer may issue a visa on the spot, he will in any case forward the record of interrogation to the department, which will verify it by checking parts of the applicant's record with diplomatic posts appropriately located. In the case of a Russian architect who wished to visit the United States in the early 1930s the Berlin consulate general took a deposition and issued a visa after receiving negative answers to such questions as: "Are you a member of the Communist Party? Would you like to be a member of the Communist Party?" The department asked the consulate in Riga to verify the applicant's employment and residence histories. With appropriate care the consulate reported what it could learn of the individual in question, and went on to identify by address and occupation the six other persons of the same name who lived in Moscow and the three who lived in Leningrad.[10]

Visa work thus requires investigative and interrogatory skill. For decades, to people of many countries, the United States has appeared as the land of opportunity, and some individuals desire to emigrate to the United States more than they desire anything else in the world. A consular officer issuing visas can expect to be deceived, not just by misstatements but by elaborate charades designed to convince him of a visa applicant's qualifications for entry into the United States. One American consul investigating the background of a prosperous shopowner was invited to the man's place of business and shown his books to convince him that the fellow was so well off that he would never become a public charge in the United States or even want to stay there and leave behind his thriving business. Only by shrewd questioning did the consul discover that the shop was not the applicant's and that the business ledgers shown him were false, made up for the occasion by an accountant hired by the applicant.

The work of issuing visas requires a good deal of courage. J. Theodore Marriner was one of the most remarkable young members of the State Department staff in Washington during the 1920s and beyond question could look forward to a career of high authority, probably an assistant secretaryship, surely an ambassadorship. It became necessary however that he should go out to the field to experience the problems and difficulties of local representation before he should spend more time in the department supervising the men and women in the field. He was assigned as consul general in Beirut. One day a local Lebanese came in and asked for a visa, and after some thought Marriner denied it. "Ted" Marriner, the individual who was scheduled for authority, was shot dead on the spot.

Visa applications, one should also relate, can lead to tragedies not merely for single individuals but for hundreds, thousands, even tens of thousands of people. In the same decade, the 1930s, issuing visas and enforcing American immigration restrictions brought considerable trouble to diplomatic officials. In the increasingly unwholesome climate of National Socialist Germany tens of thousands of German citizens, especially German Jews, applied for visas. Officials had the unhappy obligation to apply the extreme and unsympathetic limitations that the American Congress then maintained on immigration. Consular officers, apparently heartlessly but without recourse, enforced immigration laws, which among other things denied visas to people who were "likely to become a public charge," that is, who would arrive in the United States without resources and become dependent on welfare and assistance programs already inadequate for American needs in the midst of the Depression. Officials were obliged to ascertain the money and valuables that immigrants could carry, and whether relatives or friends in the United States would guarantee support to the immigrant. When the German government began to deny immigrants the right to take their property and money along, this clause of American immigration law became controversial, and because of its application American diplomatic officers were harshly judged both then and since, even though they were enforcing the clear mandates of Congress.

In setting out the routine responsibilities of a diplomat, responsibilities time-consuming beyond the imagination of the diplomat's countrymen at home, there is lastly the business of protection of citizens traveling or residing abroad. Protection is one of the most elemental responsibilities of a state in foreign relations. In the modern era when states have become representative of citizens rather than the property of princes, the obligation to protect the life and further the interests of citizens has become the basis for projection of state power and presence beyond national boundaries. The passport is the documentary proof of identity and citizenship that an individual carries into the hazardous and always uncertain foreign environment, the written guarantee that he is entitled to and enjoys assistance and protection of the government to which he owes allegiance. Thus, from the point of view of the United States government and citizenry, passport work possesses much greater importance than visa matters.

No ability is more fundamental to sovereignty, and to the right to govern, than the ability to protect those individuals who acknowledge allegiance, pay taxes, and perform military service, for therein is the essence of social contract. It is no accident that one of the notable foreign contretemps of Theodore Roosevelt's presidency grew out of an effort to protect a citizen who had been kidnapped in Morocco in 1904. Roosevelt and Secretary of State John Hay in undiplomatic language demanded that the sovereign of that North African state produce Jon Perdicaris alive or Raisuli the Bandit dead. The vigorous defense of Perdicaris, which made national and international headlines, arose from Roosevelt's recognition of the close connection between newly found world power and the ability to protect a citizen abroad.[11]

How important such instances of protection can be and how representative of general relations between countries was evident years later in the tragic case of Helmut Hirsch, who in the late 1930s found himself in trouble with German authorities and was sentenced to death by a secret court. For three months American officials at the highest levels attempted to save his life, but neither strong language and appeals from the secretary of state nor approaches to Hitler via some of the latter's associates known to American diplomats in Berlin availed in the increasingly difficult German-American political climate of that time. On June 4, 1937, Hirsch became the first American citizen to die at the hands of the Hitler regime.[12]

Protection seldom takes on the severity of the two instances described, which is well for both the citizens and governments involved. It would strain government relations to dispute many cases. And it would be a sorry experience for a citizen abroad if he had to experience such difficulties as kidnapping or a trial for his life before his country's representatives would help him. As it is, diplomatic officers furnish all sorts of assistance to citizens abroad, helping with innumerable small problems, assisting businessmen to establish connections and meet local regulations, generally seeing to it that Americans receive due process of law and protection of their rights under treaty or international usage whenever there is some dispute, wrongdoing, or simple misunderstanding.

The importance of the everyday work of protection and of associated consular activities makes it curious that these essential functions have remained so often unnoticed by most Americans, whose attention tends to focus on the unessential or perhaps more glamorous aspects of diplomacy. The many Foreign Service officers who specialize in consular affairs have been almost lost from sight. And even within the diplomatic establishment they have suffered from lack of status. Only recently has the "relationship between diplomatic mission and constituent posts" become a subject of study in the Foreign Service Institute and of a task force in the Department of State. Predictably and sadly, not much has come from this overdue attention—only perfunctory conclusions that there should be better coordination, that consuls should not be second-class diplomats. The present unsatisfactory situation, the vast public and even departmental ignorance of much of the work of the average diplomatic mission abroad, is not likely to change soon.

It is almost ironic that the task of protecting citizens has been so undervalued or perhaps so lightly accepted. The department complains chronically that it is the only cabinet department without a constituency, that it goes friendless to Capitol Hill each year for the battle of the bulging budget and fights bravely with right on its side but fares far less well than the other departments— Labor, Agriculture, Commerce, Defense, all the rest, which have powerful constituencies to carry the day with otherwise penurious congressmen. The diplomats are correct in saying that diplomatic work is by definition directed outward rather than distributed inward, directed abroad rather than at home, and that this circumstance can hardly change. But they are wrong, quite mistaken, when they say that their department lacks a constituency. Every passport holder is a constitutent. The supporters of the Department of State will never be organized like labor unions, farmers' associations, manufacturers' associations, chambers of commerce. But it is important for the department to realize how large its constituency really is and to take courage in that fact.[13]

5| The Traditional Tasks: Representing, Negotiating, Observing

What of those traditional aspects of the diplomat's job—representation, observation, negotiation? Have other duties superseded or overshadowed the original elements of the profession? No indeed, for despite the increasing complexity of a diplomat's tasks, those three basic functions have remained as much a part of diplomacy as in former times. A diplomat is today, as in the past, the representative of his sovereign or president or of the government officer in whom sovereignty or responsibility for foreign affairs resides. Then, he is a negotiator. He speaks with the voice of his principal and has the heavy responsibility to convey as accurately and completely as possible the messages and sometimes sentiments of his government to the representatives of the government to which he is accredited. And, thirdly, he must observe and report.

Representational duties are not as easy to perform as they may seem. The diplomat represents the person of his principal, receiving honors due his government or sovereign and showing the courtesies or, on less happy occasions, the imperatives or imperiousness, which his government may wish to express. Early authorities on diplomatic practice even urged that an ambassador should moderate his voice and manner to comport with the note or message he might read a counterpart, offering greetings warmly and warnings, threats, or complaints sternly. But traditional and legal definitions of diplomatic representation and the relationship between diplomat and principal cannot by their seeming clarity eliminate the duality of persons in the situation. Although diplomats speak for governments, they find it difficult to guard every word, especially in conversations in which personal relationships intrude. Although it is desirable and notably helpful for diplomats to develop friendships in the circles of government where they work, to construct informal channels of information and gentle influence that augment official relationships, it is impossible to avoid giving some of the same informal and unofficial information that one seeks. It is even more difficult to maintain and convey the distinction between what is informal but official and what is informal, personal, and in no way official. More than once an American ambassador has undercut his government's position in commercial or political negotiations by expressing in just such an informal way his own sympathy with demands of his momentary adversaries.

The representative who is attending clearly ceremonial occasions can encounter problems because of the duality between personal and official attitudes. One American ambassador affronted German leaders by refusing to attend National Socialist Party rallies to which most of the diplomatic corps were invited, not because he had instructions to boycott the celebrations, but because he felt great personal repugnance for the National Socialist government. His successor later received careful instruction to attend such ceremonies in the short months remaining before President Roosevelt called him home in November 1938.

A second basic task for the diplomatic establishment is the highly important work of negotiation. Great negotiations resemble the more commonly known circumstance of formal debate, at least in one important respect. As in debate, success in negotiation depends on preparation. It would be reckless to assert that without preparation one cannot succeed, but mastery of topics lends authority to argument. The success of American representatives at the Washington Naval Disarmament Conference of 1921–1922 derived from the care with which the Department of State and Secretary of State Charles Hughes had planned. Hughes' opening proposals—in which, some people said, he sank more ships than had all the world's admirals in a cycle of centuries—created their effective impression because of the knowledge Hughes displayed and which he had incorporated into suggestions. As mentioned, it is likewise a strength of Soviet diplomacy in the modern era that each Russian sent abroad must attain a mastery of international law and of international agreements that may become pertinent to relations with his host country. American diplomats experienced in dealing with Soviet representatives have commented on the immense authority in discussion that such preparation lends to Soviet statecraft.

Regular members of the State Department in staffs and offices, even officers serving at posts overseas, contribute by far the most part to the detailed labor that underlies whatever successes may accrue to special envoys. Not all diplomatic negotiations take place in prominent circumstances, and middle-level officers in the

Department of State meet with members of diplomatic missions in the United States and carry on innumerable discussions, which amount to a less elaborate form of negotiation. Every day of the week the ambassadors, ministers, and diplomatic secretaries of countries call on each other to discuss problems and projects. Big black limousines regularly carry foreign officials and dignitaries to and from the State Department's main entrance, the so-called diplomatic entrance, on C Street NW in Washington. A Spanish diplomat may come to discuss some aspect of maintenance of American air bases in his country, a French diplomat to deliver a note protesting or disagreeing with an American proposal for monetary reform or European economic integration. There are always details to work out on proposed visits of heads of state or even of foreign ministers or special envoys. Representatives of the department meet regularly, and sometimes it must seem continually, with Canadians, Russians, and Japanese on questions relating to fisheries, sealing, and whaling, and so business goes on. Diplomats come and go, asking questions, conveying messages, arguing points of law, requesting favors, and fulfilling formalities. Only the culmination of their efforts, arguments, and discussions requires top-level attention in most instances.

And lastly, the diplomats observe and report. No function has been more fundamental to diplomatic representation. Observation and reporting, so closely bound up in the diplomat's work, were the chief elements of the job in the days when permanent representation first became widespread. It was essential for princes and governments to know something of foreign conditions, attitudes, intentions, even occurrences. That need has not diminished just because it has been augmented by many other needs. Observation and reporting gave diplomats their character as "legal spies," and only the reciprocal need for reliable information could have overcome the reluctance of early states to receive foreign observers. There is virtually no limit to a diplomat's curiosity, although there are limits to an officer's responsibility in reporting in the twentieth century. In former times an ambassador in his sometimes lonely vantage collected an entire range of useful or interesting information, from court gossip to peculiarities of the personality and health of contacts, to commercial, military, internal, and external political information. One of those points, the health of foreign contacts and officials, has become a subject of extraordinary interest again in recent times, especially in relations with the communist states where even the most common information about individuals is almost as closed off from outsiders as top-secret material is in the West. People speculated for years about Mao's health, watched his public appearances, pounced eagerly on firsthand reports of people like Edgar Snow who from time to time saw the great man. (How did he look? How firm was his handshake? Did he have tremors? Walk easily? The CIA is still quite proud of having acquired Nikita Khrushchev's stool sample while he was in power but rumored to be in failing health.)

With the aid of a secretary or two, or perhaps in spite of such aid (Benjamin Franklin's private secretary in Paris during the Revolutionary War was a British spy), an emissary formerly had to acquire, evaluate, and report all varieties of information, cultivate the contacts necessary to accumulate the information, and carry on other activities necessary to maintain himself and his position. Times have changed as measured by the alterations in responsibility. Now diplomats specialize not only according to subject but according to location in both geographic and hierarchical senses if they follow the rather elaborate prescriptions of Foreign Service Institute training. In the two categories of diplomatic specialization, the differentiation between economic and political officers is both a matter of expertise and a symptom of the division of labor that occurs as organizations grow large. In the mid-twentieth century one cannot depend for economic information and analysis on casual perceptions of amateurs. National and international economics of trade and finance have become difficult subjects, in which knowledge comes only from study, purpose, and dedication. Balance of payments, balance of trade, tariff and monetary policy, transportation, exchange, innovation, transnational and multinational businesses and the laws that regulate them—all these and many more components of the complex and interrelated domestic and international economies require skilled assessment.

More than most diplomats, so-called political affairs specialists have continued to resemble the all-round generalist of former times. Political concerns encompass nearly all aspects of relations among states, and even if a political officer has no knowledge of esoteric and complicated areas he must deal with the political implications and complications that accompany them. His concerns are vast, for he has the task to render intelligible the political milieu, personalities, policies, and eventualities in his host country.

The work of the political affairs officer gives evidence of its many details but less of its difficulty. To acquire skill in learning what one needs to know to support intelligent policy in one's government is arduous enough; immensely more difficult is the business of conveying information in a way that will impress and stimulate the diplomatic establishment in Washington. The latter problem often defeats officers reporting from the field, though sometimes in seeking to overcome it observers and reporters arrive at imaginative communications.

According to current dogma, reporting has four requirements: observation of behavior; analysis or accounting for the observed behavior; appraisal or explaining the meaning and consequences of behavior observed and analyzed; and recommendation, in which appraisal is related to the "actions and operations of decision-making centers which diplomats represent." [14] In the age of scientific management, an age in which every aspect of diplomatic work has become subject to scrutiny, perhaps it is inevitable that even the most traditional diplomatic functions should be so dissected, analyzed, and categorized. But maybe in recent years the department's reformers have gone too far. Analysis can be valuable when it clarifies work and leads to better performance. The study of observation and reporting, like so many theoretically attractive aspects of the "new diplomacy," may well tend wrongly to reinforce the traditional way in which junior officers and men in the field, if they are wise, will keep their ideas and recommendations to themselves. Even so, diplomats in the field must become proficient in observation and in analysis; they must guard against intertwining objective analysis with subjective appraisal, which "tends to pre-empt policy decisions." [15] And they must be willing to recommend. The latter course may be presumptuous and therefore risky; one recalls Galbraith's summary of advice and instruction given him: "Silence is advised." But for any envoy of quality, it is necessary to think and speak out.

Diplomacy at the present time thus stands between tradition and modernity, old and new. Although the traditional description of the roles of diplomats no longer suffices to summarize foreign relations and the duties of diplomatic officers, that description has not become obsolete. The diplomat, caught between past and present, faces a future of uncertainty. But it is impossible to abolish the diplomat. Despite the extraordinary challenges of change, despite the innovations of post-1945 American foreign policy, Foreign Service officers and civil servants in the Department of State retain much responsibility and conduct much state business. Foreign relations—the contacts between governments—depend on the thousands of individuals who fill the spaces between sovereign entities and who ease the friction where these entities meet.

CHAPTER FIVE | Looking Ahead

If this essay were to follow the pattern of most critical and analytical writing on American foreign affairs, here is where the author should adumbrate the particular reforms that he believes will work where all others have failed. But that is no easy task. John Kenneth Galbraith has written that diplomacy "is a field where meaning is ordinarily disguised by words, the more words the better the disguise. It is one reason why discussion of foreign policy tends to be intellectually inferior even to the more suspect forms of sociology. Its reputation is saved principally by the circumstance that those who discuss foreign policy have a superior social position, more self-assurance, less awareness of what they do not know, and somewhat better tailoring." [1] His cynical comment is uncomfortably close to the mark, close enough to evoke diffidence in the person who would attempt prescription.

It is easy to speak and write about reform, almost impossible to effect it, and certain that results will be different than anticipated in the few cases where report passes beyond the printed page into application. Most of the reforms suggested by writers, some diplomats and some not, sound speciously easy to accomplish. Some say eliminate the State Department, or at least the old traditions of diplomacy wherein the conceits of Talleyrand and the deceits of Machiavelli intertwine in dark and secret ways. Others say eliminate the CIA, whose secrets and ways are even darker and less consonant with the spirit of a great republic. Or streamline the bureaucracy, as still other writers urge. Cut it to the bone. Select better secretaries of state. Give real power to the secretary, the department, the diplomats themselves. Ultimately, one might argue, the only sure improvement in American foreign affairs will come when Americans elect a President who devises and carries out foreign policies and foreign relations of which everyone approves. That latter course is an unlikely occurrence. It is much more probable that each succeeding President will follow the now-established pattern of attempting limited reform, finding it difficult or impossible, and then turning to his own devices. Perhaps the most anyone can hope for is an accommodation in which the department and its diplomats accept a role more limited than that to which they presently aspire, so at least the discontent, the bureaucratic infighting, the competition for attention and influence will consume less of the respective agencies' energy and resources.

1| Present Dissatisfactions

In the autumn of 1972 an article by William N. Turpin appeared in *Foreign Policy*; it spoke directly to the subject of departmental reform and accommodation. Since the author wrote with the advantage of diplomatic and bureaucratic experience, his "Foreign Relations, Yes; Foreign Policy, No" occasioned a considerable stir. In practically every office in State into which one might have wandered that fall, one would have espied a much-thumbed and underlined copy of the periodical. And small wonder. Turpin had struck to the heart of the department's and the Foreign Service's not-so-secret malaise, a concern for the role of the department and of the elite service in an era when the secretary of state and his whole department seemed outweighed and overshadowed in high-level policy and decisions. In truth, as another writer, the political scientist Warren Mason, noted about the same time in the *Foreign Service Journal,* American diplomats were in the midst of a "quiet crisis" in which the requirements for making a career in the bureaucracy clashed with the traditional manners, mannerisms, and tasks of diplomacy. In an age of bureaucratic competition in Washington the Department of State, and within it the Foreign Service, appeared to have lost control of policy in favor of the military services, intelligence community, and the National Security Council.[2]

The problem had become acute, a real crisis and not a quiet one either, during the tenure of Henry A. Kissinger as adviser to President Nixon for national security affairs. The successive surprises and triumphs of Nixon-Kissinger diplomacy had not only imposed sweeping policy changes from the top, both in attitudes and in the structure of relations, but had come so obviously without the knowledge, advice, agreement, or participation of the people who thought they should be defining foreign policy. It was a time when the repute of the department and the prestige of a once proud elite service fell to a low probably not reached since Senator Joseph R. McCarthy "discovered" 205 (or whatever the number was) communists and fellow travelers within State's stately corridors. Everywhere around the country and in the international press people wondered about Secretary of State William P. Rogers—about what kind of man could remain secretary while being so upstaged by Kissinger—and concluded that Rogers and the department he headed had become weak, truly effete, in ironic demonstration of the real meaning of a word long applied to caricature diplomats—a department, a secretary, a service exhausted, unable to respond to the changing world with appropriate ideas. In such a climate, with Kissinger and Nixon conducting secret negotiations in fulfillment of "secret plans" only hinted at during the 1968 presidential elections, with Rogers being a nice guy and occasionally signing ceremoniously some document resulting from labors of the peripatetic H.A.K., the diplomatic establishment confronted stark questions about its function, use, and future. What were all the striped-pants boys doing while

Kissinger, the President, and a handful of aides were doing all the "real work"?

Turpin's attempt to clarify the role of the diplomatic establishment, especially the Foreign Service, was no abstract exercise, and his nontraditional answers to the questions posed by the style and successes of the Kissinger-NSC era deservedly inaugurated discussion. And it was perhaps a good beginning to answering difficult and pressing questions in a way that might resolve some aspects of the morale crisis as well, a beginning for further attempts to define the tasks of the foreign affairs department in the context of questions and doubts that persisted even though Kissinger in 1973 accepted formal as well as *de facto* responsibility for American foreign affairs.

Turpin rightly observed that much of the morale problem in the Foreign Service and much academic criticism of American foreign policy derived from the conviction that there had been a Golden Age in which the Department of State, and more especially the secretary of state, had controlled foreign policy and provided the President's principal advice. There was widespread agreement to a contention popular among American diplomats: When advice in foreign policy comes from outside the department, it is undemocratic, sinister, threatening to American institutions.

Turpin noted the fundamental difference between foreign policy and foreign relations. The former, he said, "connotes matters between states which affect, to a significant degree, their power relationships," the latter the "normal functioning of relations" between them.[3] Because politics is about power, he argued, foreign policy since World War II has often been considered in Washington as national security policy and will always, and should always, command the attention of the President. At the same time the President will never have the time or even the inclination to conduct or direct foreign relations on any large scale.

Confusion arose when a situation developed national security dimensions or, in Turpin's words, "impinges on the President's sphere of power."[4] When that happened, and especially when it resulted in crisis, professional diplomats routinely in charge of foreign relations had to expect to be pushed aside by higher officials, by men with political and not just bureaucratic responsibility for American security and interests. As Turpin related, at the time of the Dominican crisis in 1964 the Dominican desk officer said: "On Friday I was Dominican Desk Officer; by Friday night Rusk was; and by Sunday noon Lyndon Johnson was." [5] Turpin believed such a sequence reasonable and admonished the Foreign Service to recognize that it had neither responsibility nor in all probability the ability to devise policy and to make the highest-level decisions affecting power among nations. It did have unparalleled capability to handle the enormous range of day-to-day adjustments among nations, and to do so with an expert ability, experience, and general professionalism that the President's men would never match. The time had come, he concluded, for the department men in Washington and the Foreign Service abroad to stop feeling sorry for themselves because individuals outside the corps so evidently had the big ideas, and instead to make themselves masters of the realm of foreign relations, in which policy eventually would have to be executed.

Such sensible arguments did not completely allay the desire of the professionals to make policy, nor did it provide a clear statement of work categories and responsibilities in American diplomacy. Despite his intention to show the differences between policy and relations, he began with a mistaken, or at least an imprecise, account of the two activities. Undeniably, national security may be enhanced or diminished both in policy-making and in carrying out policy. Turpin introduced the subject of security in those areas, which led to some confusion.

In dealing with security issues and foreign relations one must begin with the proposition, perhaps the realization, that foreign affairs and national security affairs are not identical. Much that takes place in American foreign affairs and much that occurs in the world has no influence whatsoever on American security. Much in foreign affairs that does eventually possess importance for national security cannot be anticipated, for it stems from trivial or routine matters unobserved in their beginnings. One can never know from moment to moment what significance some routine affair may suddenly acquire. Conversely, it is obvious that national security depends on a myriad of domestic as well as foreign factors. To the confusion of logicians and bureaucrats, scholars and diplomats, the public and the Presidents, foreign affairs and national security are both greater and lesser than each other, neither one superior or encompassing except in moments of crisis.

From this realization one can proceed to consider foreign affairs in its constituent parts—as foreign policy, foreign relations, and in the modern age perhaps in a third and much-touted component, crisis management. The first part, foreign policy, is an abstraction, a formulation of ideas about, plans for, or goals in foreign relations. The State Department and the Foreign Service have yearned to monopolize policy, have spurned much of the work of the second part, foreign relations, and proven incapable of the third, crisis management. State has ended with diminished influence in policy circles, a clear minority share of government operations abroad, at best a minor share in crisis management.

These abstractions would matter little if they remained abstract, if everyone were happy with things as they are, if State Department civil servants, Foreign Service officers, and a considerable portion of the public could tolerate such a state of affairs. But hardly anyone is content with present procedures in foreign affairs except perhaps Kissinger and a few other people. In the opinion of many writers and government servants, even Presidents and advisers for national security affairs would be delighted if there were some way to make the State Department the center, the leader if not the controller, of foreign affairs.

In the midst of such general dissatisfaction there is only modest comfort in Turpin's assignment of foreign policy to the national security managers and foreign relations to the diplomats. The question remains in the minds and on the lips of the professionals in diplomacy: How can the diplomats recover or acquire preeminence in foreign affairs?

That query has been at the core of each of the postwar studies, self-studies, and reform proposals. Some of the answers to that question have received mention in the course of the present discussion, from conservative assurances that exalted old traditions and defended them as the true and only way to extreme proposals to turn diplomacy into management and to solve policy problems by personnel administration and programming. There have been still more radical proposals, calls for yet other superpolicy presidiums, but ones in which State could dominate (or on the other side of the question, presidiums in which tradition-bound State Department influence could be eliminated); suggestions that State absorb the remnants of a CIA shorn of operations; suggestions that State subject itself to a ruthless pruning of manpower in an effort to become lean and strong (the thin man inside every fat man longing to get out). Perhaps most important of all such suggestions has been that of the late John F. Campbell, who proposed that the NSC, heavily weighted with military and intelligence representatives who overbalance the lone secretary of state, should quit making foreign policy and become once again the kind of body it started out to be—a council that considers national security questions, with emphasis on "defense budget and military strategic and tactical doctrine." [6]

Yet the record of reforms and studies, attempted improvements in departmental effectiveness and influence, is sorry indeed. It is not at all one that would encourage belief that the department could alter itself substantially via massive personnel reduction and reorganization. It is even more difficult to conceive of a situation in which a weak State Department, repeatedly a loser in Washington's bureaucratic struggles, could succeed in eliminating such an important agency as the CIA or in restricting the scope of interest and activity of the National Security Council.

2| What Is to Be Done?

The successive reformers of the postwar years have been right about one of their main concerns, and perhaps that is the best place for the department to begin, if it wishes to improve its position. It will always be essential to diplomacy, new or old, traditional or managerial, to have the highest quality personnel. Poor people make a poor organization.

On that score there is much to worry about. Present attempts to align the Foreign Service with current civil libertarian concerns, to bring minority group members into the service, and to alter the standards and nature of entrance examinations have caused some older diplomats to doubt the promise of an approach that seems designed to make the corps representative of American society in the sense that it is a cross section. They believe that the diplomatic corps should represent not the average, not the cross section, but the best in our society and population. Even more worrisome was a trend that one diplomat called "the stupidization of the foreign service," a clear and statistically demonstrable decline in the raw scores of individuals who in the 1960s had taken the entrance examination, "indicating progressively lower academic preparation among those who took the test." Not only that, but for a while the numbers of people taking the examination were also on the decline, which raised the disconcerting possibility that subsequent decades would witness a "vicious cycle of fewer and fewer people of progressively lower abilities joining the government." [7] Fortunately, that trend in part reversed. Twenty-seven thousand people took the Foreign Service examination in December 1974, but scores continued low, especially among administrative and consular cone examinees.

Having good people is necessary, but it is only a first step toward effective diplomacy, for even good people must know what they are about. As things stand, there is reason to doubt that very many American diplomats possess a clear understanding of their work. One of the worst side effects of the new era of an enlarged and reorganized diplomatic establishment showed itself when diplomats began to perceive a difference between diplomacy and careers in diplomacy. That divergence opened the way to the manifold problems of personnel management, organization, and especially of morale, which have continued to afflict the Foreign Service despite postwar reforms, initiatives, reorganizations, and presidential pep talks. It may never be possible to determine when this divergence between profession and career established itself. The process in which officers either won promotion or had to leave the service, a system not unlike that in the military services, inspired officers to serious concern with their work. But, one may well ask, upon what were diplomatic officers obliged to concentrate? The answer, of course, was on winning promotion rather than being selected out, that wonderful euphemism for being cashiered or, almost as bad, staying too long in the same rank and thus signaling one's inferiority.

It became easy to describe the career in diplomacy, difficult to describe professionalism. Americans were hard pressed to define the characteristics of a diplomat or to distinguish a good diplomat from a poorer one. The brevity of American diplomatic experience, American rejection of most of the European traditions and modes in foreign relations, and the incoherence of American experience in foreign affairs all conspired to leave diplomats without traditions, without a clear understanding of their profession. Earlier standards, those of breeding, education, and manners, had sufficed not to identify good diplomats but to denote acceptable comrades and presentable representatives of one's nation. It was easy to recognize "that statesmanlike dignity of demeanor which the necessity of holding the tongue and keeping the temper, of never speaking one's real mind and preserving appearances always tends to produce in diplomats, royal personages, high government officials and butlers." [8]

With once durable standards struck down by the egalitarian effects of reform and expansion, no example of the good diplomat remained. But the question remained: What, or who, was a good diplomat? And it was possible to contend that the men who did well in the service were the good officers, the men who received the best fitness reports from superiors and who in consequence received good assignments and regular promotion. Or as an assistant secretary of state wrote, "a 'good result' is a 'good report,' and a 'good report' is a report that is approved by somebody whose approval counts. Standards of judgment are adopted not because they are relevant but because they are convenient. Government officials begin to act like the drunk who, having dropped his wallet in the Bronx, went down to Forty-Second Street to look for it because the light was better there." [9]

The confusion on this issue was remarkable. Even the organization for evaluating American diplomatic missions and officials, the Inspectorate General, has done little to formulate a statement of the qualities that characterize "good diplomacy." According to the inspectors of the Foreign Service, a good diplomat has two abilities: He gets along well with fellow diplomats, and especially with superiors; and he is a good draftsman, capable of writing reports in good English. In short, as one senior assistant to the director general has said, and as others have doubtless thought, there is no difference between being a good diplomat and being a successful bureaucrat.[10]

It is clear that somehow, ironically, the conservators of tradition fastened on aspects of elitism and personnel, and in trying to preserve those things they lost their grip on the more important traditions of work and purpose, which alone gave them justifiable title to professional expertise. In the years before the Rogers Act the confident descriptions of diplomatic work of men like Wilbur Carr, himself not a member of that charmed inner circle of social position and Ivy League education, were crucial in convincing legislators that diplomacy demanded professionals. In a few lines he could summarize the tasks in impressive terms. "We ought," he said, "to have the most competent men we can find in every place in which we are represented to protect our interests, to resist encroachments upon our rights, to further our commerce, and to protect our citizens, and prevent misunderstanding of our motives." [11] Sadly, one receives the impression today that hardly a man or woman in the State Department could as surely and aptly define his work.

It is easy to understand why young people of quality and preparation have evinced less interest in a Foreign Service career in recent years. The frustration and bitterness of the diplomatic corps have become obvious to anyone interested enough to observe. The diplomats themselves have made clear to anyone who would listen that they considered themselves far from center stage, mistreated, ignored. Small wonder that young university graduates, whether fresh out of school or already at work, at least until the great job dearth in the mid-1970s, have shied away from a department and a service convinced of its own weakness but consumed by desire for more power and prominence. Today's old hands joined the diplomatic service not only because of the aura of glamour and the promise of world travel, high society, and excitement that seemed parts of a life in diplomacy. They joined because there was work to do, important work in foreign relations. They joined because there was challenge as well as change, honor in valiant service, satisfaction in contributing to the nation's business. The diplomatic career could become attractive once again in all of those terms, both for those already in service and for those whom the service would attract. But a sense of purpose must replace the uneasiness of today's professionals.

It is here, then, that I reach a conclusion. There must be acceptance of the proposition that the work of the diplomatic professionals is the conduct of foreign relations. They must acquiesce in the making of policy by someone else, somewhere else: the White House, the military, the CIA, somewhere other than at Twenty-First and Virginia Avenue NW. There is wisdom as well as encouragement in a maxim that dates back to the days of Napoleon and Clausewitz. "Policy," it was said, "like strategy, is an art in which everything depends on execution. Everything about it is simple, but the simple is always difficult." To bridge that gap between policy conceived and policy executed; to protect citizens and their interests; to represent the state and nation honestly; these are the tasks of the professional diplomats, difficult enough to require the utmost subtlety and skill, important enough to earn for those who persevere and succeed the respect of their fellows in government and the appreciation of their constituents in the citizenry.

NOTES

Chapter One

1. Quoted in E. Wilder Spaulding, *Ambassadors Ordinary and Extraordinary* (Washington: 1961), p. 32. The occasion for the rebuke was in February 1774, when the Privy Council was angry at Franklin for having disclosed letters in which Governor Thomas Hutchinson of Massachusetts recommended severe treatment of the demanding colonials. See Franklin's own account of his embarrassment before the council in *Benjamin Franklin: A Biography in His Own Words,* edited by Thomas Fleming (New York: 1972), pp. 249–253.

2. Quoted in John W. Foster, *A Century of American Diplomacy, Being a Brief Review of the Foreign Relations of the United States 1776–1876* (Boston: 1900), p. 26.

3. *Ibid.,* p. 46.

4. *Ibid.,* p. 47.

5. Many of Franklin's biographers have used this quotation in lieu of some of the more pointed remarks he made about his female friends and women in general. It also appears in Spaulding, *op. cit.,* p. 35.

6. Francis Wharton, ed., *The Revolutionary Diplomatic Correspondence of the United States* (Washington: 1889), Vol. IV, p. 288.

7. Graham H. Stuart, *The Department of State: A History of Its Organization, Procedure, and Personnel* (New York: 1949), p. 53.

8. The original source for this quotation is the *Writings and Speeches of Daniel Webster,* 18 vols. (Boston: 1903), Vol. XII, p. 177. But this collection is found in few libraries, so that it may be more convenient to read

extracts from the note in Robert H. Ferrell, ed., *Foundations of American Diplomacy, 1775–1872* (Columbia, S.C.: 1968), p. 208.

9. This document, dated October 18, 1854, also appears in Ferrell, *ibid.*, p. 212.

10. Stuart, *op. cit.*, p. 130.

11. *Diplomatically Speaking* (New York: 1940), p. 13.

12. *Ibid.*, p. 20.

13. Wilbur J. Carr, testifying in hearings before the Committee on Foreign Affairs, 68th Cong., 1st Sess., on H.R. 17 and H.R. 6357, January 14–18, 1924, p. 129.

14. Third Assistant Secretary of State J. Butler Wright, *ibid.*, p. 57.

15. Hugh Gibson, *ibid.*, pp. 40, 41. These lines made an immediate impression. They were already being quoted in the first book on the reformed service, *The Foreign Service of the United States,* Tracy Hollingsworth Lay (New York: 1925), pp. 240, 241.

16. Lay, *ibid.*

17. *Ibid.*, p. 66.

18. "An Act for the reorganization and improvement of the Foreign Service of the United States, and for other purposes" (the Rogers Act), May 24, 1924. 43 Stat. (Pt. I) 145.

Chapter Two

1. The Rogers Act regulated affairs within the career services but did not guarantee that all the top jobs would go to careerists. There were five groups: the Foreign Service, that is, the newly integrated diplomatic and consular service; regular civil service personnel working in the department but not available for overseas duty; clerical personnel willing to work overseas, known as Foreign Service Staff members; eventually a corps of Foreign Service Reserve Officers, people with special expertise available for temporary appointments, up to five years in duration; and, of course, the political appointees.

2. Earl E. T. Smith, *The Fourth Floor: An Account of the Castro Communist Revolution* (New York: 1962), p. 211.

3. *Diplomacy for the 70's: A Program of Management Reform for the Department of State* (Washington: 1970), p. 310.

4. Hearings before the Committee on Foreign Affairs, 68th Cong., 1st Sess., January 14–18, 1924 (on the Rogers Act) (Washington: 1924), p. 97.

5. Hearings, Committee on Foreign Relations, U.S. Senate, 89th Cong., 1st Sess., March 2, 1965 (Washington: 1965), p. 19.

6. *The New York Times,* April 4, 1973.

7. Hearings before a subcommittee of the Committee on Foreign Relations, U.S. Senate, 82nd Cong., 1st Sess., on the nomination of Chester Bowles of Connecticut to be United States ambassador extraordinary and

minister plenipotentiary to India, September 22, 1951 (Washington: 1951), pp. 5, 6.

8. Hearings before the Committee on Foreign Relations, U.S. Senate, 86th Cong., 1st Sess., on the nomination of Clare Boothe Luce to be ambassador to Brazil, April 15, 1959 (Washington: 1959), pp. 6–11.

9. Foreign Service Institute, School of Professional Studies, *Syllabus: Basic Course for Foreign Service Officers* (103rd Class, August 21–September 29, 1972), p. i.

10. Foreign Service Institute, School of Professional Studies, *Foreign Service Economic/Commercial Studies Course: Program Description and Selected Bibliography,* undated, p. 1.

11. Letter from Harry Feinstein, coordinator of executive development, Foreign Service Institute, School of Professional Studies, to members of the first "Commissioning Course" for FSO-5's, undated, course beginning October 30, 1972.

12. *Ibid.*

13. Charles Frankel, *High on Foggy Bottom: An Outsider's Inside View of the Government* (New York: 1968), pp. 46, 47. John Kenneth Galbraith, *Ambassador's Journal: A Personal Account of the Kennedy Years* (Boston: 1969), pp. 44, 29, 308.

14. "Bureaucracy and Policymaking: The Effects of Insiders and Outsiders on the Policy Process," in Morton H. Halperin and Arnold Kanter, eds., *Readings in American Foreign Policy: A Bureaucratic Perspective* (Boston: 1973), p. 95.

15. *Farewell to Foggy Bottom* (New York: 1964), p. 34.

16. It is important to note that because of the low number of officers taken in at the bottom of the service, it would have been impossible annually to eliminate 5 percent. By the mid-seventies, many more than sixteen per year were being selected out. And, of course, the figures on selection out will never reflect the numbers of individuals who resigned knowing that if they did not quit, they would be discharged.

17. The first use of lateral entry into the Foreign Service came in the War Manpower Act of 1946. The De Courcy Commission in 1952–1953 also brought about some small number of lateral appointments. But Wristonization was the most important and by far the largest such phenomenon.

18. *Farewell to Foggy Bottom,* p. 288.

19. Galbraith, *op. cit.,* p. 212.

20. Halperin and Kanter, *op. cit.,* p. 95.

21. *Farewell to Foggy Bottom,* p. 163.

22. "Operation Topsy," in *Foreign Policy,* No. 8 (Fall 1972), pp. 62–85, especially pp. 62, 64.

23. Actually, State had started a PPBS in 1963, and it had failed because the Department of Defense and the Central Intelligence Agency would not cooperate in a way that made it possible to include their hidden investments in overseas embassy and mission operations. In some instances, that meant

as much as 80 percent of a mission's budget. Although this problem was less acute on the second go-around, after 1966, it has never been resolved satisfactorily.

24. William N. Turpin, "Foreign Relations, Yes; Foreign Policy, No," *Foreign Policy*, No. 8 (Fall 1972), pp. 50–61, especially p. 54.

25. John Franklin Campbell, *The Foreign Affairs Fudge Factory* (New York: 1971), p. 80.

26. *Farewell to Foggy Bottom*, p. 24.

27. *Ibid.*, p. 29.

28. Frankel, *op. cit.*, p. 85.

29. *Farewell to Foggy Bottom*, pp. 138, 139.

30. In fact, so far the Department of State has lost every case that has gone to adjudication. Hemenway remained still busy and visible—and audible—on the Washington scene. He frequently testified before congressional committees, as at nomination hearings for various persons and positions in the foreign affairs community. And he became active and prominent in the Foreign Service Association, a professional association for Foreign Service officers, which functions somewhat ineffectually as a union. Diplomats, like university teachers in most states, have yet to shrug off their embarrassment at collective bargaining and other union-like group behavior.

31. Henry Serrano Villard, *Affairs at State* (New York: 1965), p. 4.

Chapter Three

1. William N. Turpin, "Foreign Relations, Yes; Foreign Policy, No," *Foreign Policy*, No. 8 (Fall 1972), pp. 51, 52.

2. John Franklin Campbell, *The Foreign Affairs Fudge Factory* (New York: 1971), p. 72.

3. Lisle Rose makes this important observation in his fine book *The Coming of the American Age, 1945–1946: Dubious Victory: The United States and the End of World War II* (Kent, Ohio: 1973), p. 246.

4. *Ibid.*, p. 247.

5. Charles Frankel, *High on Foggy Bottom: An Outsider's Inside View of the Government* (New York: 1968), pp. 85, 86.

6. Fred Charles Iklé, *International Negotiation: American Shortcoming in Negotiation with Communist Powers*, a memorandum for the subcommittee on National Security and International Operations of the Committee on Government Operations, U.S. Senate, 91st Cong., 2nd Sess. (Washington: 1970).

7. NSC-68 was declassified in February 1975 at the request of the historian Barton Bernstein. It was then published in the *Naval War College Review*, May–June 1975, pp. 51–108. Previously, Samuel P. Huntington, in *The Common Defense: Strategic Programs in National Politics* (New York: 1961), and Paul Y. Hammond, in Warner R. Schilling, Paul Y. Hammond, and Glen H. Snyder, *Strategy, Politics, and Defense Budgets*

(New York: 1962), had filled in much of the background and content of the famous document.

8. Dean G. Acheson, *Power and Diplomacy* (Cambridge, Mass.: 1958).

9. Ellis Briggs, *Farewell to Foggy Bottom* (New York: 1964), p. 167.

10. The "taffy pull" phrase is Nicholas de B. Katzenbach's, in an address to the American Foreign Service Association, November 1966; the hospital figure of speech comes from John Kenneth Galbraith's novel *The Triumph* (New York: 1968), p. 12. Both are quoted in Campbell, *op. cit.*, p. 228.

11. Campbell, *op. cit.*, p. 17, quoting Stewart Alsop, *The Center* (New York: 1968), p. 114. Neither author mentions the real problem in the case of Guiana: CIA money was being funneled into the country through the AFL-CIO.

12. Richard M. Nixon, *U.S. Foreign Policy for the 1970's: A New Strategy for Peace* (Washington: February 18, 1970), p. 20.

13. *Ibid.*, p. 21.

14. Richard M. Nixon, *U.S. Foreign Policy for the 1970's: Building for Peace* (Washington: February 25, 1971), p. 229.

15. Richard M. Nixon, *U.S. Foreign Policy for the 1970's: The Emerging Structure of Peace* (Washington: February 9, 1972), p. 210.

Chapter Four

1. The foregoing figures, and those to follow on costs of representation, were prepared for and released to the author by the office of the director of policy planning, West European Division, Department of State. Security regulations did not permit "breaking out" the CIA's portion of the budget.

2. Beatrice Russell, *Living in State* (New York: 1959), p. v.

3. A personal letter from Bullitt to Franklin D. Roosevelt, May 1, 1935, published in Orville Bullitt, ed., *For the President, Personal and Secret: Correspondence Between FDR and William C. Bullitt* (Boston: 1972), p. 116.

4. *Promises to Keep: My Years in Public Life 1941–1969* (New York: 1971), p. 462.

5. *The New York Times*, May 12, 1953.

6. *The New York Times*, February 24, 1972.

7. W. C. Bullitt to FDR, May 1, 1935, in Bullitt, *op. cit.*, pp. 116, 117.

8. This story appeared in a paper by Theodore A. Wilson and Richard D. McKinzie, which they presented at the meeting of the Organization of American Historians in Chicago, April 12, 1973. They found the anecdote in an unpublished draft article, undated, in the papers of Ambassador Henry F. Grady, deposited in the Truman Library.

9. These figures and facts were made available to the author by Donald J. Simon, at the time head of the Record Services Division of the Department of State, and by various officers working in the Operations Center.

10. Information in the foregoing paragraph comes from several visa files

released to the author, with the provision that names and file numbers be removed to respect the legal safeguards on the privacy of individuals investigated and interrogated in the course of visa and passport work. The files are drawn from records of the 1930s and fall into the 811.11 category under the decimal filing system in use in the Department of State at that time.

11. See Thomas H. Etzold, "Protection or Politics? 'Perdicaris Alive or Raisuli Dead,'" *The Historian,* XXXVII, No. 2 (February 1975), pp. 297–304.

12. This story appears in Thomas H. Etzold, "An American Jew in Germany: The Death of Helmut Hirsch," *Jewish Social Studies,* XXXV, No. 2 (April 1973), pp. 125–140.

13. See the more extended discussion of this problem in Thomas H. Etzold, "Understanding Consular Diplomacy," *Foreign Service Journal,* March 1975, pp. 10–12; and the unpublished paper by John W. Bowling of the staff at the Foreign Service Institute, "The Relationship Between Diplomatic Missions and Constituent Posts," undated.

14. Paul M. Kattenburg, formerly on the staff of the Foreign Service Institute, "Some Comments on Observation, Analysis and Appraisal in Diplomacy," a paper prepared for the annual meeting of the American Political Science Association, Chicago, September 7–11, 1971.

15. *Ibid.*

Chapter Five

1. John Kenneth Galbraith, Statement before Members of Congress for Peace Through Law, June 27, 1972, p. 1.

2. William N. Turpin, "Foreign Relations, Yes; Foreign Policy, No," *Foreign Policy,* No. 8 (Fall 1972); Mason, "Quiet Crisis: Diplomatic Careers in Tension with Bureaucratic Roles," December 1972, pp. 17–19.

3. Turpin, *ibid.,* p. 55.

4. *Ibid.,* p. 57.

5. *Ibid.*

6. John Franklin Campbell, *The Foreign Affairs Fudge Factory* (New York: 1971), p. 268.

7. *Ibid.,* p. 142.

8. Aldous Huxley's description of Simmons, the gentleman's gentleman, quoted in Henry Serrano Villard, *Affairs at State* (New York: 1965), p. 7.

9. Charles Frankel, *High on Foggy Bottom: An Outsider's Inside View of the Government* (New York: 1968), pp. 81, 82.

10. Archer Blood, in an interview with the present writer in October 1972.

11. Wilbur J. Carr, in hearings before the Committee on Foreign Affairs, 68th Cong., 1st Sess., on H.R. 17 and H.R. 6357, January 14–18, 1924, p. 129.

SELECTED
BIBLIOGRAPHY

At the outset of this discussion of sources for the foregoing book, it is appropriate to mention once more the information, ideas, and help received in interviews, conversations, and written comments from the individuals named earlier in the Acknowledgments. Their comments were especially important for an understanding of recent and contemporary issues and problems in the American foreign affairs community. Also important for information on affairs in recent years were various articles in *The New York Times,* a newspaper that pays considerable attention to the interminable difficulties of conducting American foreign relations.

Much material of a less contemporary nature came from researches on this and other projects in the general records of the Department of State, deposited in the National Archives. This project began with a thorough evaluation of the message traffic between the Department of State and the embassies in Berlin and London from 1933 to 1939, including administrative and consular files. Indeed, all messages not restricted were perused, along with the card files on restricted messages. The idea was that in such a survey the principal components of diplomatic endeavor would show up in their actual workaday perspective. Only the good advice of colleagues has prevented the present writer from making up tables and sharing with readers the eyestrain incurred in this manner. Still, much information of use came to hand in this survey. The reading of administrative and consular files, especially, proved valuable in learning more about the actual work of foreign relations.

Several collections of private papers also figured in the preparation of this manuscript. The small collection of the papers of P. Blum, an AID official after World War II, is deposited in the library of Yale University under restrictions that did not permit citation, though they were of modest use in thinking through the problems discussed in Chapter Three. Of greater bulk and importance, the papers of Henry L. Stimson, also in the Yale University manuscripts library, contained material relevant to this endeavor as to so many others. Indeed, the Stimson collection is becoming one of the leading sources for historians of recent foreign and military affairs. At the Library of Congress Manuscripts Division the present writer read with profit in the papers of Norman Davis and William E. Dodd, both of whom served Franklin D. Roosevelt and the Department of State in the 1930s. Of premier importance in the same depository, the papers of Wilbur J. Carr improve understanding of the person who, more than any other single individual, brought about reforms in the foreign services of the United States early in the twentieth century. The present writer also used the papers of Theodore Roosevelt, John Hay, Elihu Root, and Cordell Hull, all in the Library of Congress Manuscripts Division.

The remainder of this bibliography is divided into three sections: printed documents, reports, and other materials not "published" in the bibliographer's usual sense of that term; a selection of published materials, including scholarly studies, memoirs, and collections of papers and documents, as well as articles; and finally a brief list of other bibliographies to which ambitious readers may turn for still more suggestions on sources and readings.

Public Documents, Reports, and Limited Distribution or Unpublished Items

Entries in this section are arranged alphabetically by author or originating agency. Within author groups, hearings and reports of congressional committees are in chronological order.

American Foreign Service Association. *Toward a Modern Diplomacy.* A Report to AFSA, *Foreign Service Journal,* November 1968. In a way this study was a prelude to the one sponsored and conducted officially within the department in 1970. Concerns about freedom of thought and initiative and policy power for professional diplomats showed up in both studies.

Bowling, John. "The Relationship Between Diplomatic Missions and Constituent Posts." Unpublished and undated. An instructor at the Foreign Service Institute, Bowling makes some important observations on one of the most difficult present-day problems within the establishment, a problem that touches not only on organization, but on the relative status of consuls and diplomatic secretaries.

The Brookings Institution. *Administration of Foreign Affairs and Overseas Operations.* Report prepared for the Bureau of the Budget. Washington: 1951. This was one of the first of many reports and studies recommending simplification of American foreign affairs by combining the efforts and the overseas services of the many agencies operating abroad.

Galbraith, John Kenneth. "Statement before Members of Congress for Peace Through Law." June 27, 1972. Galbraith singles out the source of recent American policy disasters as the idea that America had to fight communism in the third world, and along the way notes some of the problems of bureaucracy and organization that have made foreign affairs so difficult to control.

Guerriero, Donald, and Paul Von Ward. "The Meaning of University Training for FSO's." *The Department of State Newsletter,* January 1975, pp. 22, 23. The authors, both Foreign Service officers, concluded that university training resulted in a modest, but statistically measurable, increase in average annual salaries for officers assigned to a year of schooling at some point in their careers.

Kattenburg, Paul M. "Some Comments on Observation, Analysis and Appraisal in Diplomacy." A paper prepared for the annual meeting of the American Political Science Association, Chicago, Ill., September 7–11, 1971. Before his retirement from the Foreign Service, Kattenburg spent many years teaching at the Foreign Service Institute. His paper shows some of the less attractive aspects of an over-intellectualized, over-structured approach to diplomatic work.

Kissinger, Henry. "The Department of State and the Foreign Service." A speech at the swearing-in ceremony of the 119th Foreign Service Officer class, June 27, 1975. Kissinger tried to convince the incoming young officers that they would have a "central place in the policy process."

Nixon, Richard M. *U.S. Foreign Policy for the 1970's: A New Strategy for Peace.* Washington: February 18, 1970. The first of Nixon's annual "State of the World" messages to Congress on American foreign policy, this document and its successors are essential reading for students of foreign affairs and foreign affairs administration during the Nixon presidency.

————. *U.S. Foreign Policy for the 1970's: Building for Peace.* Washington: February 25, 1971.

————. *U.S. Foreign Policy for the 1970's: The Emerging Structure of Peace.* Washington: February 9, 1972.

————. *U.S. Foreign Policy for the 1970's: Shaping a Durable Peace.* Washington: May 3, 1973.

U.S. Congress. *Congressional Record.* Volumes 64, 65, 72, and 92. The volumes enumerated contain the debates on the three great pieces of twentieth-century legislation affecting the organization of professionals of the Foreign Service—the Rogers Act of 1924, the Moses-Linthicum Act of 1931, and the Foreign Service Act of 1946.

————. Act of May 24, 1924 (43 Stat. 140). The Rogers Act, as remarked in the text, established the combined Foreign Service and placed entry and promotion on strict examination and merit bases. It also raised salaries and provided a retirement system for Foreign Service officers.

————. Act of February 23, 1931 (46 Stat. 1207). The Moses-Linthicum Act raised salaries again and reorganized the classification system of diplomatic clerks. Most important, perhaps, though seldom remarked, was Section 31 of the act, which attempted to break up the informal but powerful old-boy clique, which influenced the distribution of top positions. Section 31 prohibited members of the Foreign Service Personnel Board from being promoted to minister or ambassador for at least three years following service on the board.

————. Act of August 13, 1946 (60 Stat. 999). This act replaced the Rogers Act with new provisions on personnel organization, salary and retirement system revisions, and new promotion regulations. It also created the Foreign Service Institute for in-service education and training of officers.

U.S. Department of State. *Biographical Register.*

————. *The United States Consular System: A Manual for Consuls and also for Merchants, Shipowners and Masters in their Consular Transactions; comprising the Instructions of the Department of State in Regard to Consular Emoluments, Duties, Privileges, and Liabilities.* Washington: 1856.

————. Secretary of State's Public Committee on Personnel. *Toward a Stronger Foreign Service. A Report to the Secretary of State.* Washington: 1954. This is the famous report of the Wriston committee, recommending enlargement of the Foreign Service by amalgamation with a number of people within the State Department and in the field, as well as many other recommendations in personnel management and organization.

————. Committee on Foreign Affairs Personnel. *Personnel for the New Diplomacy.* New York: 1962. Christian A. Herter served as chairman of this committee, which recommended improvement of American foreign affairs by development and use of specialists within the diplomatic service.

————. *Diplomacy for the Seventies: A Program of Management Reform for the Department of State.* Washington: 1970. The compilation of the reports of thirteen task forces organized within the Department of State, the volume stresses the need for creativity, openness, and sound management in the department and especially in the Foreign Service.

————. "Schedule of Courses at the Foreign Service Institute." *Department of State Newsletter,* November 1975, pp. 36, 37.

————. *Vienna Convention on Diplomatic Relations and Optional Protocol on Disputes.* Washington: 1961.

U.S. General Services Administration. *Government Organization Manual.* Washington: published annually.

U.S. House of Representatives. *Report from the Committee on Foreign Affairs, amending Senate resolution 1345, for the reorganization of the consular service; with hearings.* March 14, 1906. (House report 2281, 59th Cong., 1st Sess.)

————. *Report on the inspection of U.S. consulates in the Orient.* March 28, 1906. (House document 665, 59th Cong., 1st Sess.). This lengthy report details the dishonesty and drunkenness of far too many American agents in the Far East.

————. *Hearings on the Improvement of the Foreign Service,* before the Committee on Foreign Affairs. March 20, 1912. (Hearings on House resolution 20044, 62nd Cong., 1st Sess.)

————. *Report to accompany House resolution 20044, Improvement of the Foreign Service.* June 5, 1912. (From the Committee on Foreign Affairs, 62nd Cong., 1st Sess.)

————. *Hearings before the Committee on Foreign Affairs on House resolution 12543, for the Reorganization and Improvement of the Foreign Service of the United States.* December 11–19, 1922. (67th Cong., 4th Sess.)

————. *Foreign Service of the United States, hearings on House resolutions 17 and 6357 for the reorganization and improvement of the Foreign Service.* January 14–18, 1924. (68th Cong., 1st Sess.) This is the single most important set of hearings on the Rogers Act in its various legislative incarnations.

————. *Reorganization and Improvement of the Foreign Service of the United States, a report to accompany House resolution 6357.* February 4, 1924. (House report 157, 68th Cong., 1st Sess.)

————. *Modern Communications and Foreign Policy.* June 13, 1967. (House report 362, 90th Cong., 1st Sess.)

U.S. Senate. Committee on Foreign Relations. *Reorganization of the Foreign Service, a report to accompany House resolution 13880.* February 28, 1923. (Report no. 1142, 67th Cong., 4th Sess.)

————. *Subcommittee of the Committee on Foreign Relations on the Nomination of Chester Bowles to be U.S. Ambassador Extraordinary and Minister Plenipotentiary to India.* September 22, 1951. (82nd Cong., 1st Sess.) This and other nomination and confirmation hearings cited below are rich in both information and anecdote.

————. *Hearing before the Committee on Foreign Relations on the Nomination of Maxwell H. Gluck to be Ambassador to Ceylon.* July 2, 1957. (85th Cong., 1st Sess.)

————. *Hearing before the Committee on Foreign Relations on views of*

Acting Secretary of State Christian Herter on the Nomination of Maxwell Gluck to be Ambassador to Ceylon. August 1, 1957. (85th Cong., 1st Sess.)

————. *Foreign Service Appointments, Hearings before the Committee on Foreign Relations.* January 27, 1959. (86th Cong., 1st Sess.) This hearing has several interesting items on the status and proportion of women in the Foreign Service and on the foreign language capabilities of American diplomats, who are much maligned for inadequacy in the latter respect.

————. *Hearings before the Committee on Foreign Relations on the Nomination of Clare Boothe Luce to be Ambassador to Brazil.* April 15, 1959. (86th Cong., 1st Sess.)

————. *Committee on Foreign Relations: Hearings on the Nominations of Walter Annenberg, Jacob Beam and John S. D. Eisenhower.* March 7, 1969. (91st Cong., 1st Sess.) Annenberg's question-and-answer period is of special interest in the context of the personal expenses that fall to ambassadors sent to the more illustrious European capitals.

————. *Hearing before the Committee on Foreign Relations: State Department and Diplomatic Nominations.* March 2, 1965. (89th Cong., 1st Sess.)

————. *International Negotiation: American Shortcoming in Negotiating with Communist Powers.* A memorandum for the Subcommittee on National Security and International Operations of the Committee on Government Operations. 1970. (91st Cong., 2nd Sess.)

————. *Negotiation and Statecraft.* Subcommittee on National Security and International Operations of the Committee on Government Operations. 1970. (91st Cong., 2nd Sess.)

Wilson, Theodore A., and Richard D. McKinzie. "White House versus Congress: Conflict or Collusion? The Marshall Plan as a Case Study." A paper presented at the annual meeting of the Organization of American Historians, Chicago, Ill., April 12, 1973.

Books, Articles, and Published Documents

Acheson, Dean. "The Eclipse of the State Department." *Foreign Affairs,* Vol. 50, No. 4 (July 1971), pp. 593–606. Here Acheson remarks "the attraction of foreign affairs to anyone who has easy access to the president" and points to such whims and ways as an important reason for the declining policy influence of the State Department.

————. *Power and Diplomacy.* Cambridge, Mass.: 1958. In this book Acheson states with some brevity and eloquence the views of national power and security that made him loom so large in the confused and some-times frightening years of the early cold war.

———. *Present at the Creation.* New York: 1969. This memoir contains much incidental information on the changing role of the State Department and various persons in high politics as concerns the formulation and con-duct of American foreign policy following World War II.

Adams, Charles Francis. *The Works of John Adams, Second President of the United States.* 10 volumes. Boston: 1850.

Almond, Gabriel. *The American People and Foreign Policy.* New York: 1960. This small volume is already a classic on American popular attitudes and opinions on and toward foreign affairs and diplomacy.

"Are Diplomats Necessary?" *Punch,* April 28, 1970, pp. 588–599. This series of brief articles is typically irreverent, typically British (very), and quite funny, a welcome diversion from the ponderous language of bureau-crats and social scientists, which characterizes so much of the literature on modern foreign relations.

Attwood, William. *The Reds and the Blacks.* New York: 1967. Former Ambassador Attwood describes the complexities of conducting American foreign relations in Africa during the Kennedy and Johnson presidencies, years in which the Chinese were attempting to woo African clients away from both Americans and Russians.

Bacchus, William I. "Diplomacy for the 70's: An Afterview and Appraisal." *American Political Science Review,* Vol. 68 (1974), pp. 736–748. This article contains intelligent comment on the Department of State's self-study of 1970, and on the consequences as well as lack of consequences in the first years thereafter.

———. "Obstacles to Reform in Foreign Affairs: The Case of NSAM 341." *Orbis,* Vol. 18 (1974), pp. 266–276. Another installment in this author's evaluation of why nothing seems to change in State.

Barnett, V. M., Jr., editor. *The Representation of the United States Abroad.* New York: 1965. The essays in this volume were originally published in 1956 and then revised for the later edition. They emphasize repeatedly the contrasts between traditional tasks and issues in foreign affairs and those of the rapidly changing 1950s and 1960s. Of particular interest is Howland H. Sargeant's contribution, "American Information and Cultural Represen-tation Overseas," pp. 75–128.

Beaulac, Willard L. *Career Diplomat: A Career in the Foreign Service of the United States.* New York: 1964. In this easy-to-read contribution to the Macmillan series of "career" books, Ambassador Beaulac commences with the sage observation that "the two most important decisions a man ever makes are his selection of a profession and his choice of a wife, and that the first is based on ignorance and the second on emotion." His book shows throughout a similar mixture of wisdom and experience.

Bemis, Samuel Flagg. *John Quincy Adams and the Foundations of American Foreign Policy*. New York: 1949. In reading this unsurpassed study of JQA, it is difficult to know who more deserves admiration, the awe-inspiring Adams or his estimable and accomplished biographer.

———— and Robert H. Ferrell, editors. *The American Secretaries of State and their Diplomacy*. 18 volumes to date. New York: 1927–1970. Since this series first appeared, it has been a valued starting point for students of the diplomacy of the various secretaries, and it still serves that function today. In fact, in recent years the series has shown a noteworthy improvement in quality, with especially fine volumes on Marshall, Acheson, and Dulles.

Blancké, W. Wendell. *The Foreign Service of the United States*. New York: 1969. The former ambassador has written an informative, though not exciting, survey of the foreign affairs establishment of the 1960s and has embellished it with a modicum of earlier history.

Bohlen, Charles E. *The Transformation of American Foreign Policy*. New York: 1969. Out of his forty years of experience as a Foreign Service officer, Bohlen argues for the adequacies rather than the inadequacies of American foreign policy and takes particular care to avoid blaming military men for what may have gone wrong: "I can think of no single decision that has ever been taken by the American military contrary to the wishes of the constituted civilian authority. All the mistakes we made—and indeed we have made them—have been made by the civilian authorities."

Bowers, Claude G. *Chile Through Embassy Windows: 1939–1953*. New York: 1958. After fourteen consecutive years as ambassador to Chile, Bowers wrote this paean to Chilean democracy and included, of course, some anecdotes about his life and work and the many prominent Americans and Chileans with whom he dealt. Perhaps most interesting are his observations that women rule Chile behind the scenes, of which Bowers seemed to disapprove.

Bowles, Chester. *Ambassador's Report*. New York: 1954. Chester Bowles has a special facility for weaving together personal and humanly interesting material with the larger observations on American and world affairs that he wishes to convey. In this volume he "reports" on his first tour as ambassador to India.

————. *Promises to Keep: My Years in Public Life 1941–1969*. New York: 1971. With the same qualities of authorship remarked in the preceding entry, Bowles discusses his remarkable progression from one important job in public service to another. This volume is especially interesting for his recounting of his time as Kennedy's undersecretary of state for political affairs, during which Kennedy and Bowles tried—and mostly failed—to bring about large changes in the organization and style of American foreign affairs.

Brenner, Michael J. "The Problem of Innovation and the Nixon-Kissinger Foreign Policy." *International Studies Quarterly,* Vol. 17, No. 3 (September 1973), pp. 255–293. This essay, though dated by its focus on the Vietnam involvement, remains one of the most thoughtful critiques of Nixon-Kissinger leadership. It is important in the context of the present study because of Brenner's concern about policy innovation and leadership.

Briggs, Ellis. *Farewell to Foggy Bottom.* New York: 1964. Briggs' own wit and verbal cleverness sometimes seem to lead him into disdain for outsiders who do not understand the problems and issues of conducting American foreign relations. And he is unashamed to be of the old school and opposed to modernization of his former profession. One should not allow the emphatic arrogance of his pronouncements to obscure the common sense and experience that underlie his judgment.

Bullitt, Orville, editor. *For the President, Personal and Secret: Correspondence Between FDR and William C. Bullitt.* Boston: 1972. Although the correspondence is flattering to neither of these remarkable men, it is full of anecdotal material and shows as well the common interweaving of mundane with transcendent matters.

Burke, Lee H. *Ambassador at Large: Diplomat Extraordinary.* The Hague: 1972. In recent years the title "ambassador at large" has been devised for those individuals whom Presidents may wish to use in a combination of formal and informal ways as FDR did with Harry Hopkins. Burke looks at the tradition of presidential appointment of special agents and more closely at the handful of men who have so far held this exalted title. The volume is somewhat less informative than one might have hoped.

Byrnes, James F. *Speaking Frankly.* New York: 1947. This brief memoir has proven of durable interest for students of postwar American foreign affairs.

Campbell, John Franklin. *The Foreign Affairs Fudge Factory.* New York: 1971. The author's years as a junior Foreign Service officer made him somewhat impatient, even bitter. But these attitudes do not blunt the impact of his thoughtful criticism not only of State, but of the foreign affairs and intelligence communities.

Childs, J. Rives. *American Foreign Service.* New York: 1948. In this book Minister Childs set out to describe the service, the profession, and the embassy work of American diplomats in the aftermath of the great Foreign Service Act of 1946. As Joseph C. Grew noted in the introduction to the volume, it thus was a successor to the book by Tracy Hollingsworth Lay, which had attempted a similar task following passage of the Rogers Act in 1924. There is a definite "old boy" tone to the book.

Clark, Eric. *Diplomat: The World of International Diplomacy.* New York: 1973. This curious book debunks the mystique that has grown up around diplomacy. "The problem of the world's diplomacy at the moment is that it is still constructed as though diplomats were dealing with great events. . . ." The book is not systematic in its review of the state of world diplomacy, but it is refreshing.

Craig, Gordon, and Felix Gilbert, editors. *The Diplomats, 1919–1939.* 2 volumes. Princeton, N.J.: 1957. Though somewhat dated, the essays in these volumes contain information and evaluations of the persons and policies prominent in the interwar diplomacy of the powers and should not be overlooked.

Crane, Katherine. *Mr. Carr of State: Forty-seven Years in the Department of State.* New York: 1960. Though not strong in analysis, this book reads well and contains much information of use. Readers may wish to see Robert H. Ferrell's entry on Carr in the *Dictionary of American Biography.* Serious researchers will need to use the Carr papers and associated materials.

Curtis, George T. *Life of Daniel Webster.* Vol. II. New York: 1870. This old volume contains one of the first, and most extensive, attempts to sort out the complicated questions surrounding the authorship of the notorious Hülsemann Note. It is grand reading besides.

Daniels, Josephus. *Shirt-Sleeve Diplomat.* Chapel Hill, N.C.: 1947. Daniels was proud of his willingness to work hard, if necessary in his shirt sleeves, and he accomplished much in his time in Mexico. But it is important to realize that the style of shirt-sleeve diplomacy in the early twentieth century differed vastly from that of the middle nineteenth century.

Davies, John Paton, Jr. *Foreign and Other Affairs.* New York: 1964. Acutely critical of American foreign policy as the 1960s wore on, Davies identified a new grouping in public affairs—the radical center—and mocked the "realist" pretensions of the foreign affairs establishment. This is a clever, though bitter, book.

De Conde, Alexander. *The American Secretary of State: An Interpretation.* New York: 1962. De Conde emphasizes the personal attainments and the personal nature of the influence of the secretaries of state over the decades. It is not a profound book, but it is engaging and worth perusal.

"Diplomatic Method." 11 articles in the *International Journal,* Vol. XXX, No. 1 (Winter 1974–75), published by the Canadian Institute of International Affairs. This is an interesting attempt to compare diplomatic method at present in a number of countries, with emphasis on the English-speaking states of the West. The essays deserve some attention, as does the periodical.

Dodd, William E., Jr., and Martha Dodd, editors. *Ambassador Dodd's Diary 1933–1938.* New York: 1941. Dodd does not show up much better in his diary than he did in his work, but the diary does illustrate the manifold concerns of day-to-day diplomatic work.

Etzold, Thomas H. "An American Jew in Germany: The Death of Helmut Hirsch." *Jewish Social Studies,* Vol. XXXV, No. 2 (April 1973), pp. 125–140. This story illustrates the importance as well as the frustration of routine protection work. It has the added dimension of being the case of the first American citizen to die by order of the National Socialist government under Adolf Hitler.

————. "Protection or Politics? 'Perdicaris Alive or Raisuli Dead.' " *The Historian,* Vol. XXXVII, No. 2 (February 1975), pp. 297–304. The article stresses the diplomatic rather than the political party dimensions of the case and argues that the former far outweighed the latter in leading to the famous Roosevelt-Hay message to the sultan of Morocco.

————. "Understanding Consular Diplomacy." *Foreign Service Journal,* March 1975, pp. 10–12. This essay suggests that the Department of State has a large constituency and a large responsibility to it through performance of consular services and functions. In addition, the article details and criticizes outmoded reasons for the snobbery that still leads to denigration of consular work and consuls in comparison with political affairs and officers.

Ferrell, Robert H., editor. *Foundations of American Diplomacy, 1775–1872.* Columbia, S.C.: 1968. Here one can find excerpts from a number of documents important in American foreign affairs in the first century of American independence, documents accompanied by an exceptionally good interpretive introductory essay.

Foster, John W. *A Century of American Diplomacy, Being a Brief Review of the Foreign Relations of the United States 1776–1876.* Boston: 1900. In one of the first attempts to write a survey of American diplomatic history, Foster showed an engaging respect for tradition as well as wide acquaintance with the documentary sources available in his day. Then the writing of a "textbook" was not a matter of using secondary or scholarly literature nearly so much as of reading the journals and papers of Congress, the early editions of papers relating to foreign relations, and the like. An attractive, unabashed national pride also marks the volume. Present-day students of American foreign affairs ought to read it.

Frankel, Charles. *High on Foggy Bottom: An Outsider's Inside View of the Government.* New York: 1969. A professor of philosophy, Frankel has combined journal entries from his time in State with intelligent reflections on the nature and value of American cultural diplomacy. His is a mature and thought-provoking book.

Galbraith, Catherine A. "Mother Doesn't Do Much." *Atlantic Monthly,* May 1963. Reprinted in John Kenneth Galbraith's *Ambassador's Journal* (see next entry), pp. 529–541. Reading this lively account of the labors that fall to a diplomat's wife and family is enough to tire one immediately. It leaves one wondering little why Catherine Galbraith may have become ill in India.

Galbraith, John Kenneth. *Ambassador's Journal: A Personal Account of the Kennedy Years.* Boston: 1969. Galbraith's ego and his appreciation for pretty women show strongly in this volume ("The more underdeveloped the country, the more overdeveloped the women"), as do his wit, intelligence, and observational abilities. There is something to be said for appointing compulsive writers to embassies, for Galbraith's extensive diary-keeping has resulted in an unusually full account of his life as ambassador to India.

Griscom, Lloyd C. *Diplomatically Speaking.* New York: 1940. Of all the memoirs the present writer has read, Griscom's is the most amusing; and for its reconstruction of the life and times of turn-of-the-century America and life abroad, the volume is unparalleled.

Halberstam, David. *The Best and the Brightest.* New York: 1969. The heavy irony of the title does not quite make up for deficiencies in analysis, but the book does contain anecdotes and details about many of the people who made and/or interfered with American foreign policy and diplomacy in the Kennedy years.

Harr, John E. *The Anatomy of the Foreign Service: A Statistical Profile.* New York: 1965. The manipulation of numbers and statistics is thankless work and almost always seems somewhat uninspired, yet Harr's work repays close reading.

―――. *The Development of Careerism in the Foreign Service.* New York: 1965. This study is regrettably inadequate.

―――. *The Professional Diplomat.* Princeton, N.J.: 1969. This is a superior treatment from political science and sociological perspectives of the modern American foreign affairs establishment. It lacks sound historical perspective, concerns itself too little with how things should be, and falls into the mode so well described by John Campbell in his discussion of how observers sometimes begin to think that understanding bureaucracy is more important than changing it.

Hartmann, Frederick. *The New Age of American Foreign Policy.* New York: 1970. Part Two of this thoughtful book contains a series of chapters on policymaking, including some attention to problems of organization and personnel in recent times.

Hulen, Bertram D. *Inside the Department of State.* New York: 1939. This journalist's account was for some years much quoted and referred to. It is difficult for a reader today to understand why.

Hunt, Gaillard. *The Department of State: Its History and Functions.* New Haven, Conn.: 1914. A longtime worker in the Department of State, Hunt wrote the first history of that organization. He had edited the Journals of the Continental Congress and other early journals of the United States Congress and drew almost solely on them for the early part of his book. His history began with the preparation of a pamphlet of the same title for the department's exhibit at the Chicago World's Fair of 1893. Though dry, the book still possesses a modest usefulness.

Huntington, Samuel P. *The Common Defense: Strategic Programs in National Politics.* New York: 1961. This is a landmark book in national security studies and has material of interest on the formation and contents of NSC-68 as well as on the movement of and play for policy power in the post-World War II national security-foreign affairs community.

Ilchman, Warren Frederick. *Professional Diplomacy in the United States 1779–1939: A Study in Administrative History.* Chicago: 1961. Ilchman's study practically overflows with information, though it is dryly written and not strong enough in analysis. Everyone who researches and writes in this field does, however, need to use it.

Jackson, Henry M., editor. *The Secretary of State and the Ambassador: Jackson Subcommittee Papers on the Conduct of American Foreign Policy.* New York: 1964. In highly distilled format, these papers contain an extraordinary number of sensible observations on the work and position of modern American ambassadors. These are essential reading.

————, editor. *The National Security Council.* New York: 1965. Though useful, these papers are less impressive than those relating to ambassadorial functions.

Kennan, George F. *Memoirs.* 2 volumes. Boston: 1967, 1971. These volumes show the mind and attitudes of an elitist, and it is a disquieting picture. There is intellect, to be sure. There is also arrogance, impatience, and snobbery.

Lay, Tracy Hollingsworth. *The Foreign Service of the United States.* New York: 1925. This book was the first to celebrate and describe the newly created Foreign Service as established by the Rogers Act. A consul general, Lay reviewed at some length the issues and pressures that had presaged reform. His book remained the standard work and reference until the Foreign Service Act of 1946 changed important features of the order.

Leacacos, John P. *Fires in the In-Basket: The ABC's of the State Department.* Cleveland, Ohio: 1968. Bemoaning the fact that "The lounge-chair diplomat has succeeded the armchair strategist and the Monday-morning quarterback," Leacacos pronounced the American public woefully ignorant of the State Department, foreign affairs, and current events. He set out to write a "primer" on the making and conduct of foreign policy and produced an interesting, though overlong and overwritten essay.

Lisagor, Peter, and Marguerite Higgins. *Overtime in Heaven: Adventures in the Foreign Service.* Garden City, N.Y.: 1964. Here are a handful of adventure stories starring various individuals from the diplomatic services. This volume has good pace and makes fine light reading.

Marrow, A. J. *Making Waves in Foggy Bottom.* Washington: 1974. This short book by a consultant in management psychology celebrates the success of a managerial revolution in the Department of State, a celebration that may be both misguided and premature.

Martin, John Bartlow. *Overtaken by Events: The Dominican Crisis from the Fall of Trujillo to the Civil War.* New York: 1966. In his long memoir, former Ambassador Martin displays a judicious temperament and keen reportorial ability.

Mason, Warren L. "Quiet Crisis: Diplomatic Careers in Tension with Bureaucratic Roles." *Foreign Service Journal,* December 1972, pp. 17–19. Mason commented perceptively on some of the stresses he observed while visiting the department as a participant in the State Department-sponsored Scholar-Diplomat Seminar program.

Mattingly, Garrett. *Renaissance Diplomacy.* Baltimore: 1955. This classic volume has perspectives on the traditions and crafts of diplomacy from which every student of such affairs can profit. In addition, it is gracefully written.

McCamy, James L. *The Administration of American Foreign Affairs.* New York: 1950. In this rather dated volume, the writer focuses on "the administration of foreign affairs in terms of the organization of government, the people who do the work, and the consequences of the work done by people in the organization." There are a number of shrewd observations here, written in a style that curiously combines briskness with slightly florid metaphors ("subtle poisons").

———. *Conduct of the New Diplomacy.* New York: 1964. This book is not only brisk but incisive and even controversial. Some examples: "The Department is too much dominated by career Foreign Service officers: remember that this group is not chosen or trained to work at foreign policy but only at foreign relations . . ." and, "We can rule out the lunch hour as time for planning. Usually nothing but indigestion is produced in Washington luncheons."

Miller, Hope Ridings. *Embassy Row: The Life and Times of Diplomatic Washington.* New York: 1969. A society columnist, Ms. Miller has understandably oriented her book toward gossip, goings-on, parties, and the like.

It does contain a number of good anecdotes and is pleasant reading. Did you know that when Khrushchev visited the United States in 1959 no one mentioned the normal limits of official hospitality, so that he brought along fifty persons and 824 trunks and suitcases?

Millis, Walter, editor. *The Forrestal Diaries.* New York: 1951. These reflective writings, excellently edited, have much material on the development of integrated military and foreign policy following World War II.

Mosher, Frederick C. *Democracy and the Public Service.* New York: 1968. Like John E. Harr, Mosher was drawn into consultation and participation in the studies and self-studies of the State Department throughout the decade of the 1960s. This volume, a series of lectures, focuses not on the State Department itself, but on the problems of public administration and public service in American governance.

Murphy, Robert. *Diplomat Among Warriors.* New York: 1964. In this excellent memoir Murphy shows little or no sign of the bitterness over policy power that marks so many experienced diplomats. In part that is probably because as FDR's personal representative, Murphy did wield influence and was close to power. The book remains one of the best among the many entries in memoir literature.

Nicolson, Sir Harold. *Diplomacy.* Third edition. New York: 1963. First published in 1939, this treatise by an eminent diplomatist and historian has deservedly been read, admired, and used by students and professionals of every Western nation. Now it is dated; and it always lacked comprehensive applicability to American diplomacy, since Americans early departed from strict adherence to the forms and traditions of European usage. Yet the essay is wise, engaging, literate, and informative, and readers of the present day should not overlook it.

————. *The Evolution of Diplomatic Method.* New York: 1954. Here Nicolson published four lectures on the evolution of classical European diplomacy, with some mention of the prominence of the United States in shaping international intercourse following World War II. He concluded: "Now that the old disciplines of Pope and Emperor, the old correctives of the Concert of Europe and the Balance of Power, have been dispensed with, it is regrettable that the authority exercised by the United States is not more consistent, convincing and reliable. Yet I am not pessimistic about the evolution of their diplomatic method. I know that the Americans possess more virtue than any giant Power has yet possessed . . . they are astonishingly quick at digesting the experience of others. And, I believe that the principles of sound diplomacy, which are immutable, will in the end prevail, and thus calm the chaos with which the transition between the old diplomacy and the new has for the moment bewildered the world."

Palmer, Margaret. "Man Ought to Looke a Given Horse in the Mouth." *Foreign Service Journal,* February 1975, pp. 6–10. The wife of a retired ambassador, Ms. Palmer discusses with wit and good humor the departmental regulations on receiving personal gifts, and cleverly introduces a number of vignettes illustrative of the trials for Foreign Service families abroad.

Pearson, Drew, and Constantine Brown. *The American Diplomatic Game.* New York: 1935. After dedicating the book "to the pawns in the game," Pearson and Brown decried stridently the failure of American and world leaders to create a peaceful order after World War I, then predicted with absolute certainty that war would come to Europe and the Far East within five years. There are the usual anecdotes and reconstructed conversations, now familiar hallmarks of the Pearson style.

Perkins, Dexter. *The American Approach to Foreign Policy.* Cambridge, Mass.: 1952. Here one of the grand old men of American diplomatic history sets out with vigor and approbation the moral and intellectual elements of the American diplomatic tradition.

Phillips, William. *Ventures in Diplomacy.* Boston: 1952. Billy Phillips belonged to that inner coterie in the old diplomatic and Foreign Service school. He began his professional career as a student interpreter in Peking about 1906, in the last days of Manchu China. His memoir has withstood the tests of time and use.

Platt, D. C. M. *The Cinderella Service: British Consuls since 1825.* Hamden, Conn.: 1971. First published in Britain by Longman's, this book received rather bad reviews. Yet it is interesting for the similarities of problems, complaints, and movements for reform in the British and American diplomatic and consular services of the late nineteenth and early twentieth centuries. There are undoubtedly errors in the Platt book; but it is far more useful and better reading than reviewers would lead one to believe.

Plischke, Elmer. *Conduct of American Diplomacy.* Third edition. Princeton, N.J.: 1967. Plischke's textbook is virtually the only approximately current such guide to American practice now that Graham H. Stuart has passed from the scene.

————. *United States Diplomats and Their Missions: A Profile of American Diplomatic Emissaries since 1778.* Washington: 1975. This book consists of a few observations based on manipulation of the data in a publication of the State Department entitled *United States Chiefs of Mission, 1778–1973,* published in Washington in 1973. Some curious statistics emerge from the exercise, but the results *in toto* are not substantial.

Queller, Donald E. *The Office of Ambassador in the Middle Ages.* Princeton, N.J.: 1967. This is an excellent study of the origins of modern Western diplomacy, with much fascinating information on Venetian law and practice.

Ransom, Harry Howe. *Central Intelligence and National Security.* Cambridge, Mass.: 1958. Perhaps the first careful study of the conflict created by the establishment of the Central Intelligence Agency in the National Security Act of 1947, this book has remained an important commentary on the contradictions surrounding secrecy in a democracy as well as on the role of intelligence in security and foreign affairs.

————. *The Intelligence Establishment.* Cambridge, Mass.: 1970. Ransom's second book is the best single assessment of the place of intelligence and intelligence agencies in American public and foreign affairs.

Roetter, Charles. *The Diplomatic Art: An Informal History of World Diplomacy.* Philadelphia: 1963. This breezy book is lots of fun. Examples: "Hermes was the patron of ambassadors and heralds, also of vagabonds, thieves and liars"; "What divides the professionals from the 'amateurs' is generally not expertise, but the right to a pension"; and, commenting on the fast-increasing number of nations playing in and at world diplomacy: "Some countries are fast running out of diplomats. Iceland gave up the unequal struggle long ago. Its representation on a number of international organizations dealing with defense, social matters, economics, and culture in the Western hemisphere is in the hands of one solitary diplomat. But then, of course, no matter what the context of the meeting or the agenda, Iceland is concerned with only one question—herrings."

Rostow, W. W. *View from the Seventh Floor.* New York: 1964. Rostow became head of the Policy Planning Council in the State Department in December 1961, and here presents some of his big ideas on force and foreign relations, United States interests, relations with countries in various geographical regions, and other broad topics in foreign and security affairs. The book recalls the extent to which Rostow was a genuine cold warrior.

Russell, Beatrice. *Living in State.* New York: 1959. Bea Russell and her Foreign Service officer husband, Earle (Jr.), were surely among the more optimistic, energetic, and adventuresome people in the service in the late 1950s. Her written remembrances virtually sparkle with enjoyment of life, and one recalls with regret, though with a certain sense of the appropriate, that Earle Russell, Jr., should have died while driving across the desert in the kind of headlong trek that he loved.

Schilling, Warner R., Paul Y. Hammond, and Glen H. Snyder. *Strategy, Politics, and Defense Budgets.* New York: 1962. This volume contains three enduringly important essays on post-World War II development of integrated foreign and security affairs. They are, in fact, essential reading.

Schulzinger, Robert D. *The Making of the Diplomatic Mind: The Training, Outlook, and Style of United States Foreign Service Officers 1908–31.* Middletown, Conn.: 1975. In this revision of his Yale dissertation, Schulzinger has produced a finely drawn intellectual portrait of one of the most important generations of American professional diplomats. The book shows both good writing and solid research.

Seward, Frederick W. *Reminiscences of a War-time Statesman and Diplomat 1830–1915*. New York: 1916. Frederick Seward was never a statesman, and not much of a diplomat, but he was his father's son and assistant secretary of state. His memoir is silly, but useful for appreciating the tone of his times.

Simpson, Smith. *Anatomy of the State Department*. Boston: 1967. In a book that caused quite a stir upon its publication, Simpson criticizes the department and his former colleagues for failure to think big and perform energetically and laments the scarcity of "imaginative diplomatic operators."

Smith, Earl E. T. *The Fourth Floor: An Account of the Castro Communist Revolution*. New York: 1962. The former ambassador to Cuba has written one of the longest I-told-you-so's in the diplomatic literature, and blames everyone he can think of for all that may have gone wrong in American policy toward Cuba and Castro in the late 1950s and early 1960s.

Spaulding, E. Wilder. *Ambassadors Ordinary and Extraordinary*. Washington: 1961. This book is known to and used by everyone writing in this field. It is one of the most lively compilations of anecdotes on this subject, with no particular pretension to analysis, but with a measure of sophistication and a sense of proportion.

Stanton, Edwin F. *Brief Authority: Excursions of a Common Man in an Uncommon World*. New York: 1956. This common man had a sharp eye and ear, so that he remembered and recounted stories that illuminate the actual work of diplomatic representatives abroad. Good sense and assimilated experience show throughout the memoir.

Steiner, Zara S. *Present Problems of the Foreign Service*. Princeton, N.J.: 1961. In this brief study, the author calls for less snobbery and more expertise in the Foreign Service, the common prescription for reform in the late 1950s and early 1960s.

————. *The State Department and the Foreign Service: The Wriston Report—Four Years Later*. Princeton, N.J.: 1958. After noting that rapid implementation of the Wriston proposals had led to a rigidity in rules and procedures, Steiner advocated increased bottom-level recruitment, a more careful selection of ambassadorial appointees, and improvement in the method of obtaining officers with functional expertise.

Stimson, Henry L., with McGeorge Bundy. *On Active Service in Peace and War*. New York: 1948. This quasi-memoir is particularly interesting for its information on the decisions and issues of politico-military affairs at high levels during and at the close of World War II.

Stuart, Graham H. *American Diplomatic and Consular Practice*. Second edition. New York: 1952. Though this book is far out of date, it will probably never be surpassed in its treatment of traditions and past practice.

Stuart combined broad knowledge with clear writing and exceptional skill at organizing his subject.

————. *The Department of State: A History of Its Organization, Procedure, and Personnel.* New York: 1949. This history is informative, thorough, and sound, as well as entertaining; and it is particularly handy as a quick reference on the general history of the department.

Thayer, Charles W. *Diplomat.* New York: 1959. Thayer never quite decided whether to write an American treatise on diplomacy, as Sir Harold Nicolson had done for European diplomacy, or to write a memoir and criticism of the American diplomatic establishment. The book does some of all, not enough of any. It is still entertaining to read because of the sharp wit and pen of the author.

Trevelyan, Humphrey. *Diplomatic Channels.* Boston: 1973. A veteran British diplomatist, Trevelyan displays the acerbic wit that makes British public school stereotypes immediately recognizable—and to American audiences, amusing. He has some noteworthy observations on his profession, among them: "Policy, like babies, used to be made casually, in response to immediate urges or needs. Now everything, from families to foreign policy, is planned"; and more practical for his confreres, "a diplomat should . . . above all, seek to pack the department with his friends. If he achieves this, he need have no thought for the morrow. His peccadilloes will be suppressed before they come to the ears of ministers perennially nervous of the press; his errors of judgement will be forgotten; his unfulfilled prophecies will be lost in the files: all will be given unto him."

Turpin, William N. "Foreign Relations, Yes; Foreign Policy, No." *Foreign Policy,* No. 8 (Fall 1972), pp. 50–61. Although this article has had much influence in the foreign affairs community, readers should know that at least some academic observers disagree with necessarily distinguishing between policy and relations. See Ronald J. Stupak and David S. McLellan, "The Bankruptcy of Super-Activism and the Resurgency of Diplomacy and the Department of State," *Foreign Service Journal,* April 1975, pp. 23–28.

Tuthill, John W. "Operation Topsy." *Foreign Policy,* No. 8 (Fall 1972), pp. 62–85. Tuthill makes the case for the value and effectiveness of management about as well as it can be made. Certainly his personal accomplishments are praiseworthy, and his experiences make interesting reading.

Van Deusen, Glyndon G. *William Henry Seward.* New York: 1967. Seward was an exceptional figure in American politics of the middle nineteenth century, and not only a strong and sometimes wild secretary of state. This fine biography affords an opportunity to become acquainted with a remarkable person, though one difficult to understand and impossible to predict.

Varé, Daniele. *The Laughing Diplomat.* New York: 1938. In defining diplomacy, Varé remarked that "sometimes you work at a Foreign office, but mostly you live abroad, write reports, and go to dinners, and make love to pretty women." He was one of the cosmopolitans of his day, an old China hand, and a willing servant of Il Duce, Mussolini. He was in addition a diarist, shrewd, and a man of wit and humor. His is a languidly elegant memoir.

Villard, Henry Serrano. *Affairs at State.* New York: 1965. More than a storyteller, Villard was an emissary of much good sense. With humor rather than bitterness, he has recalled some of his experiences and pointed up foibles in the American way of conducting foreign relations. Perhaps his views were summed up best in one quotation from François de Callières: "The prince should further remember that it is within his power to equip the able man with all the necessary means, but that it is not in his power to endow with intelligence one who does not possess it."

Warwick, Donald P. "Performance Appraisal and Promotions in the Foreign Service." *Foreign Service Journal,* July 1970, pp. 37–41, 45. This article is a well-thought-out variation on the idea that unless people know what their superiors expect of them, and are rewarded when they perform as expected or required, they will probably be confused and less effective than they could be. This obvious but important idea still has not made enough headway in the State Department.

————. *A Theory of Public Bureaucracy: Politics, Personality, and Organization in the State Department.* Cambridge, Mass.: 1975. This book is one of the results of a study commissioned and then almost canceled by the State Department as high officials vacillated in their support for management reform in the late 1960s. It is by far the most readable and intelligent of the numerous studies of bureaucracy in State and deserves careful reading.

Wharton, Francis, editor. *The Revolutionary Diplomatic Correspondence of the United States.* 6 volumes. Washington: 1889.

White, Andrew D. *Autobiography of Andrew Dickson White.* 2 volumes. New York: 1905. Another longtime diplomat, White left one of the fullest and most charming remembrances of life at the top in late nineteenth-century America.

Williams, Benjamin H. *American Diplomacy: Policies and Practice.* New York: 1936. This was one of the first full-scale attempts to prepare a political science textbook on American foreign relations. It had a heavy emphasis on foreign economic relations and singled out the Department of State and the Foreign Service among all other federal agencies as "the road builders on the way to peace."

Wriston, Henry M. *Diplomacy in a Democracy.* New York: 1956. After heading up the blue ribbon commission to recommend reforms in the State

Department, Wriston wrote a modest essay stressing the importance of diplomacy and diplomats. His essay is more rhetorical than analytical.

Bibliographies of Merit

Blancké, W. Wendell. *The Foreign Service of the United States*. New York: 1969. Ambassador Blancké has helpfully listed all the major legislation on the organization of American diplomatic personnel from the American Revolution to the time of his book's publication.

Harmon, Robert B. *The Art and Practice of Diplomacy: A Selected and Annotated Guide*. Metuchen, N.J.: 1971. Drawing on books and periodicals in French, German, Spanish, English, and occasionally Russian, as well as on government documents and serials, Harmon has compiled a long and in some ways interesting bibliography, though his method and criteria of selection are in no way discernible. The effect is slightly disconcerting.

Harr, John Ensor. *The Professional Diplomat*. Princeton, N.J.: 1969. As one might expect, this excellent book contains many references to important documents, books, and articles.

Plischke, Elmer. *Conduct of American Diplomacy*. Third edition. Princeton, N.J.: 1967. This quasi-textbook has many useful bibliographical suggestions. Plischke has long been a prominent authority on American diplomatic practice and has a thorough acquaintance with the literature.

―――. "Research on the Administrative History of the Department of State," in Milton O. Gustafson, editor, *The National Archives and Foreign Relations Research* (Conferences of the National Archives Series). Columbus, Ohio: 1975, pp. 73–102. The notes to this article are jam-packed with citations to documents, books, and articles of considerable utility. The essay itself ought to be required reading for any person thinking of undertaking writing or research in the administrative history of the State Department.

Schulzinger, Robert D. *The Making of the Diplomatic Mind: The Training, Outlook, and Style of United States Foreign Service Officers 1908–31*. Middletown, Conn.: 1975. This fine analysis has perhaps the most extensive single bibliography among the works cited in the present manuscript. In keeping with the focus of the book, the bibliography is oriented toward the early part of the twentieth century.

Stuart, Graham H. *The Department of State: A History of Its Organization, Procedure, and Personnel*. New York: 1949. Stuart was a scholar of the old order, which meant among other things that he was thorough. His bibliography contains citations to a number of books now little read, partly because they are old, partly because many libraries do not have them. But the old volumes often contain much information and anecdote that repays reading, and so one should not overlook the possibilities listed here.

Warwick, Donald P. *A Theory of Public Bureaucracy: Politics, Personality, and Organization in the State Department.* Cambridge, Mass.: 1975. The bibliography of this book is particularly helpful for references to social science literature on bureaucracy, organization, administration, and management.

INDEX

ABOUT
THE AUTHOR

Thomas H. Etzold is a professor of strategy at the Naval War College, Newport, Rhode Island. He received his B.A. and M.A. degrees at Indiana University, and his Ph.D. at Yale. He is co-editor, with F. Gilbert Chan, of a volume in the History of Modern China series, *China in the 1920s: Nationalism and Revolution,* published by New Viewpoints in the fall of 1976.

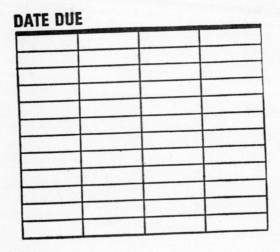